THE BIBLE
CALLS FOR ACTION

THE BIBLE
CALLS FOR ACTION

BY GEORGE D. YOUNGER

PHILADELPHIA

THE JUDSON PRESS

CHICAGO   LOS ANGELES

PRINTED IN THE U.S.A.

FOREWORD

THE BIBLE CALLS FOR ACTION was written to meet a need long felt by those interested in the relation of biblical faith to the problems of our complex modern society. There were, to be sure, many books that dealt with the application of Christian truths to social problems. These fell into two categories: those which emphasized analysis of the problems that confront contemporary society, and those which, by means of texts drawn largely from the prophets, but also to a lesser extent from the Gospels, attempted to construct a biblical foundation for social concern. Neither kind met the need for an examination of biblical teaching to discover whether or not it contained a mandate for social action.

After a long search the Rev. George D. Younger was asked to undertake the task. There were many reasons for the choice. Among them were his proven skill in the use of those tools necessary for biblical study and interpretation, his broad, firsthand acquaintance with contemporary theological thinking, his experience in an urban pastorate, where he has emphasized the application of the Christian faith to social, industrial, and political questions, and his skill in expression, attested by his able editorship of *Foundations: A Baptist Journal of History and Theology* and by his articles in the fields of theology and social criticism.

That the choice of an author was wise will be verified by a careful reading of this volume, the unique feature of which is its willingness to let the Bible speak for itself. The author's primary concern has been to make clear the biblical viewpoint or perspective and to let it stand in judgment upon contemporary thought and action. This approach is

3

the more attractive because of its originality. The author is not held captive by any one school of thought. He writes freely, courageously, and independently.

This book is intended for those who find themselves involved in the task of developing a program of social study and action in the local church and are concerned that their program be based on Bible teachings. The suggestions listed as guides for meditation and the questions designed as springboards for thought and discussion should prove valuable for group use. Though written primarily as a guide for group study, the book should prove equally useful to individuals seeking a more adequate understanding of the Scriptures and their relation to contemporary life.

Some readers may find themselves confronted with viewpoints with which they do not at once agree. If, however, they persist with open minds, they will find themselves grappling with some of the basic elements of biblical religion as these stand in judgment on twentieth-century life. They are apt to emerge from the experience with their horizons considerably expanded. This, at least, is the hope of those whose interest in the book has made its publication possible.

JOHN W. THOMAS, *Executive Secretary*
Council on Christian Social Progress
The American Baptist Convention

New York
January 10, 1959

CONTENTS

5

PREFACE

IF THE CHRISTIAN LIVED HIS WHOLE LIFE within the fellowship of the Christian church and if God had arranged for the church's life to be hermetically sealed from all the rest of life, there would be little need to consider the question of Christian social action. All of his responsibilities to his fellows would be met if he would merely "love the brethren," and the large life of the world outside would have little influence on his life of cozy fellowship. But anyone who looks with half an eye at the real situation of the Christian church knows that this is not the case.

By its very nature as a missionary fellowship, the Christian church is called to go outside its own walls and meet the citizen of the world where it finds him, where he lives an everyday life and does everyday things. Many a church has found that it could not begin to speak to him of the love of Christ until it was able to show that this love caused it to speak directly to his questions of housing or work or local politics. And even the sheltered round of church activities is not exempt from the same problems that agitate the wider society. We see our churches failing to surmount barriers of race and class, acquiescing at every turn of United States foreign policy and generally proving that, even within the Christian fellowship, the Christian faith does not seem to make much of a difference.

The command, "Go into all the world and preach the gospel to the whole creation" (Mark 16:15), means exactly what it says. The Christian church is called to live the most important part of its life at the edge of its fellowship, at the tangent where the life of the church touches the life of the world. Today, it is repeatedly being said that "the church

7

is mission." And the church shows itself to be alive and missionary only when it is constantly moving out beyond its own boundaries to reach deeply into the lives of men, showing in word and deed that it represents a crucified and risen Savior.

In times past it would have been unthinkable to mention evangelism and social action in the same breath. Proponents of the "personal gospel" and those of the "social gospel" each believed that their own views must preclude the others', and no one ever asked whether the position of either represented the whole gospel. But time has moved along, and we are now being forced to recognize that the fullness of the Christian faith requires that both these activities be carried out in alliance with each other. Culbert G. Rutenber has stated this clearly in *The Reconciling Gospel*, the 1961 study book for the Schools of Evangelism: "Christian social action is a form of witness to the love and lordship of Christ . . . . social action *is* evangelism in one of its important forms."[1]

The kind of evangelism which concerned itself only with the mathematical process of adding souls to the ranks of the redeemed has shown that it can be quite out of touch with the realities of the world when, for example, a nationalist revolution is making all things new in one of the recently born nations or when a sophisticated secular culture is saying to the churches in America, "Take care of the kids in Sunday school, but don't try to say anything about how mother and father spend Saturday night." It is equally true that the concept of social action which saw every new trend in the social sciences or politics to be the wave of the future has shown itself to be equally out of touch with the eternal purposes of God. It has not shown men how to protest when a communist government was seeking to bring every

[1] From *The Reconciling Gospel*, by Culbert G. Rutenber, pages 124, 128. Copyright, 1960, by The Judson Press, Philadelphia.

aspect of human life under its sway. And it has often found
its voice muted when social reforms like public housing and
social security, that were supposed to have heralded the dawn
of a new era, have turned out to have their own peculiar
problems and to have created their own share of human
misery. Now we know that Christian social action is an
important part of Christian witness, but, nevertheless, only
a part.

Something more than the mere practical situation in which
the church finds itself should move it to social action. The
very nature of the gospel itself calls Christians to witness
by deed as well as by word. As stated in the title of this
book, "The Bible Calls for Action." For too long the Bible
has been read as if it made no such call. Instead of impelling
the Christian out into the life of the world, Bible reading
has too often given him only a sense of solace and comfort.
He has looked on it as a storm shelter, not realizing that
what it really contains are marching orders.

This book is an invitation to the reader to examine the
faith that is in him. If he is a person who has been greatly
involved in political and social action, he is invited to examine himself to see if his action has proceeded from the
fullness of his faith. If he is a person who has been greatly
involved in affairs of the church, he is invited to search himself to see why his faith has not resulted more often in effective political and social action. And if he is a person who
has made no great ventures in the sphere of action or of
faith, he is invited to confront the limitless dimensions of
the life Christian.

Some will be using this book in classes and groups. Others
will be reading it for themselves. The author would suggest
that all use it in the following manner:

1. Prepare yourself in prayer before reading a chapter.

2. Read the chapter through in one sitting, if at all possible. If some passages seem difficult to understand, do not stop too long over them but mark them to come back to later.

3. Read for yourself the central passages from the Bible on which the chapter is based, as given in the section, "For Your Personal Meditation and Study."

4. Go on to consider the questions, "For Thought and Discussion," along with any other questions that may have been raised in your mind by what you have read.

Some will feel that this book is not specific enough in describing the actual task of social education and action in a local church and community. This is because the book has been intended from the start to be a discussion of the *basis* for Christian social action, not a handbook of techniques. To keep your own thinking close to the actual problems we face in social education and action, it will be well to take a specific area (for example, race relations, labor-management relations, or international affairs) and, after reading each chapter in this book, consider what that chapter has added to your understanding of the way in which Christians must deal with problems in the area you have chosen.

You are being invited to examine the faith that is in you, in the hope that it will grow deeper and more active through being confronted with the faith set forth in the Bible.

1

THE BIBLE'S POINT OF VIEW

EVERY ONE OF US has a point of view that influences the way we look at life and the way we act. Our point of view has been formed by a great many influences—family, school, church, community, work. But now it is our own point of view, as much a part of us as the color of our hair or the accents of our voice. This does not mean that our point of view cannot be changed; but to change it requires us to know ourselves and criticize ourselves more deeply than most of us are willing to do.

The Bible, too, has a point of view, a perspective from which it reports and judges the events of man's life. In the Bible we are brought face to face with our God, and its pages speak to us of the wonderful ways in which he has dealt with men. To read the Bible and to meditate upon it is to find our own point of view brought into sharp contrast with the Bible's point of view. In the light of God's revelation, we discern our weaknesses and shortcomings, our false assumptions and prideful excesses; we know our need to change.

In our churches social education and action has not received[1] the emphasis given to other areas of the church's life—worship, evangelism, Christian education, missions, stewardship. Most church members have paid little attention

[1] The singular verb is used advisedly, for education and action are but complementary aspects of the *one* social program.

11

as Christians to questions of legislation, community action, daily work, and the like. Many reasons may be given for this state of affairs, but the deepest reason seems to be that we have not understood that the Bible calls for action.

We all need to go back and study our Bible more closely. When we do so, we shall begin to understand that Christian social education and action has its place in the purposes of God. This book invites you to look at the Bible and discover for yourself how large and important a place this is. You are invited to examine your own point of view and the Bible's point of view in order to help you understand that *the Bible calls for action.*

GOD AND NEIGHBOR—FACTS OF LIFE

Man can never escape the rule of God and the society of his neighbors—this is the essential point of view of the Bible. Nowhere is this made clearer than in Jesus' choice of the greatest commandments in the Law of Israel (Mark 12:28-34):

> "Hear, O Israel: The Lord our God, the Lord is one Lord; and you shall love the Lord your God with all your heart, and with all your soul, and with all your strength" (Deut. 6:4).
> "You shall love your neighbor as yourself" (Lev. 19:18).

Jesus told his listeners, "There is no other commandment greater than these."

"You shall love the Lord your God. . . ." We stand always in relation to God as his creatures, his subjects, his children. It is easy to live as if the only things that count in life are the things we can see. Today's America is a land where it is perfectly possible to live as if God did not exist. Those who live in urban areas, surrounded on all sides by the works of man, sustained by the labor of countless workers, and completely separated from the working of nature, may feel no need to look outside human society for their

sustenance or their support. But the faith of the Bible knows that over and above the visible world there stands an invisible God, who has made, rules, and loves this world.

Here is the ground of our life—in God. And the basic reason for us to be concerned about the life of the world is not because it is so important for our own existence, but because it is important to God. Civil war in a far country, surpluses on America's farms, high prices eating into a worker's take-home pay, residents on a local street refusing to welcome a Negro family—all these are part of the world God rules. They are as much a part of this world and of God's concern as are the mission efforts of our churches, the national crusades for prayer and church attendance, even our own devotions with him in the secret place. There is no distinction between the "sacred" and the "secular" in God's eyes, because the whole life of the world is lived in relation to him.

"You shall love your neighbor. . . ." Although the Bible often speaks of private devotions and the life of the soul, Jesus was true to the Bible's essential point of view when he lifted from the obscurity of the miscellaneous laws in Leviticus this passage about the neighbor. The Bible continually says that we have others who depend on us and who influence us, our neighbors in society who also live under God's rule. Most people are willing to admit their relation to God, but continue to think of religion as "a personal thing" between themselves and God. They are overlooking the other half of the Bible's perspective, love for our neighbors as well as for God. We must not only acknowledge God, but also remember that we live in a society and have neighbors near and far.

In modern life we have become completely dependent on each other. The self-sufficient, lonely life of the homesteader and woodsman has given way to the dependent life of urban masses. Yet, in spite of our great need for each other in even the smallest details of life, we keep to ourselves and cherish the illusion that all that matters in life happens within our own skin or inside the four walls of our home. This is not only false to the realities of life; it is false also to the point of view of the Bible. In the Bible, as a present-day Bible scholar has said, "One man is no man." Man is never alone, but always depends on the fellowship of his neighbors.

It has taken the wonders of radio and airplanes and the stresses of world war and international revolution to show us in the modern world a fact which should have been clear even in the time when Rome ruled all the known world. Our neighbor is not just the person next door or in the next town. As Wendell Willkie told us, we live in "one world," and the person who lives in the islands of Indonesia or the plains of Russia or the mountains of Paraguay is also our neighbor. This is the way God made the world, but it has taken modern technology to make this fact plain to us.

No man can think of himself as living alone. God and neighbor—these are the two great facts of life for the Christian. He can do nothing in his life without taking them into account. While the man who does not acknowledge God's rule may look at his own life and all the swirling events in the world around him as if they were the playthings of chance or the result of man's efforts, the Christian always sees that "behind the dim unknown standeth God within the shadow" keeping watch over his children and his world.

MAN CREATED IN SOCIETY

We are so accustomed to thinking of ourselves entirely as individuals with our own rights and wills, that we often forget that the Bible knows little or nothing of this way of looking at life. When God made the world, he made man as a social being and set him in society with his neighbors from the very beginning:

> "Then God said, 'Let us make man in our own image, after our likeness; and let them have dominion over the fish of the sea, and over the birds of the air, and over the cattle, and over all the earth, and over every creeping thing that creeps upon the earth.' So God created man in his own image, in the image of God he created him; male and female he created them" (Gen. 1:26-27).

The word "man" in our English Bibles is *Adam* in the Hebrew. Adam, the first man, is also *Adam*, "the man" or mankind. The Bible recognizes that man was created for society. When God created Adam, he made mankind; when God created "him," he created "them"; when God made man, he was making male and female. In the act of creation God formed human society. He made sure that man would never be alone, but would always live in close connection with his fellows.

We are accustomed to making distinctions between what is "personal" and what is "social." But the biblical way of looking at ourselves cuts completely across this kind of distinction; we are both persons and members of society. Adam is Adam, the first person, who knows himself by name and can be addressed individually and can act for himself. But Adam is also *Adam*, the first member of society, who cannot live without fellowship and who depends on all others.

Modern social psychology has discovered much the same truth about man; namely, that there is no sharp dividing line between the personal and the social. Our first awareness of our own individuality comes through interaction with our family and others in society. Much that we think to be distinctive about ourselves is the result of the influence of the society in which we live and the social groups to which we belong. It is too simple to say that we are basically individuals with personalities all our own or that we are basically members of society with nothing to call our own. We are a complex in-between; we are both Adam and *Adam*.

Human society has been given a special place in the world. The man (*Adam*) was to have "dominion" or rule over all the natural world, even though he was a creature like all the rest of the creation. "Thou hast made him a little less than God, and dost crown him with glory and honor. Thou hast given him dominion over the works of thy hands; thou hast put all things under his feet. . . ." When outsiders criticize church people for thinking too highly of man when he is only a speck compared with the vastness and mass of the universe, the only answer we can give is that this is the way the Lord made it. Man and his affairs have special importance in the universe not because we wish it to be that way, but because God has made it that way.

MAN, A LIVING SOUL

Another important fact about ourselves which the Bible assumes but which we have often neglected is that we are whole persons, not creatures who are half-spirit and half-matter. Again the story of Creation gives us the clue:

> "Then the Lord God formed man of dust from the ground, and breathed into his nostrils the breath of life; and man became a living being" (Gen. 2:7; KJV, "a living soul").

Here again it helps to know the original Hebrew in which the Old Testament was written. The word *nephesh* means both "breath" and "soul." When God formed man out of dust, he did not *give* him a soul; he breathed his breath into him and he *became* a soul. All through the Bible it is assumed that man is a soul.

How different this is from our usual way of looking at ourselves! Whereas, in much of our thinking we have differed little from the pagan Greeks, who thought of man as having a natural body that was inhabited by a pale, invisible shadow known as the soul, the Bible says that we cannot draw a line between soul and body; we are all soul. This means that when we act, it is not as if a mind moved by a soul made our body respond with action. Instead our whole being—brain, nervous system, muscles, emotions, and all—acts at the same time. No division can be made between the "physical" and the "spiritual." They are all part of the whole.

We often assume in our churches that our task is to minister to men's "spiritual needs" while other agencies take care of the "physical needs." When we say this, we are being false to the Bible, which makes no such distinction. If man *is* a soul, it makes a difference "spiritually" when he is hungry or oppressed or deprived of love and status, just as it makes a difference "physically" when he is out of touch with God or lost in some form of immorality. There is no line of division in the life of a man. Every one of us is a whole person; we live our lives with our whole being.

Our churches are quite accustomed to giving up their proper concern for the whole life of men by allowing themselves to be classed as "spiritual" institutions concerned only with "spiritual" matters. Social action is then limited to "moral" issues affecting the purity of the believers—issues like alcohol, gambling, and vice—or is given a minor place as one of the secondary concerns of the minister, the official boards, and the congregation. Recognizing that every person is a "living soul" should cause a church to question these false assumptions about social action. The fact that a member is unemployed or unemployable is of as great concern to his welfare as his church attendance. The elimination of racial segregation in the community is of as deep concern to the church as the maintenance of Christian education. And the work of our national ambassadors and businessmen in foreign countries should be followed by the churches as closely as they follow the work of our foreign missionaries. The narrow boundaries of the "moral" and "spiritual" cannot contain the work of God or of his Church, if man is truly whole, a living soul.

THE CONSEQUENCES OF SIN

There is one further fact about ourselves which the Bible remembers at all times: we all are involved in sin. The story of what happened in the Garden of Eden (Gen., chap. 3) is not only about a man, Adam, and a woman, Eve; it is a story about all mankind, and it involves each and every one of us. God created mankind as good. Man was to have a special place in the world, enjoying full fellowship with his fellows and with God. The significance of the story of the tree and its fruit is that man rebelled against his Creator and set himself up in the place of God:

"Then the Lord God said, 'Behold, the man has become like one of us, knowing good and evil'" (Gen. 3:22).

The story of Adam is the story of the human race. We have strayed from our Creator and tried to live as if we were in complete control of our destinies and our world.

All human life is lived with the consequences of sin. As Adam was expelled from Paradise and forced to live a hard life among his fellows, so we live as exiles from God. We are alienated also from our fellow men. We share the eternal loneliness of Cain as "fugitives and wanderers on the earth"; we know the confusion of Babel where each cannot truly understand the other's speech. Our relations with both God and our neighbor are disrupted by sin.

Here again we find that the Bible's point of view is different from the way we are accustomed to looking at things. When we talk about "sins" we usually mean the personal transgressions we commit out of pride or immorality or ignorance. But our "sins" are the result of our "sin." It is our rebellion against God and our distance from him and our neighbors that are the misery of man. Most of that which we call "sin" is the consequence of sin, the refusal to acknowledge that we have been created by God and live under his rule.

To some people it may seem as if the fact of sin in our lives means that God has let the world slip from his fingers. If God is truly good, they argue, he would not allow evil and misery and pain to continue to exist in the world. But the Christian view of sin never attributes it to God's will; sin is the result of man's free will, the disobedience of Adam re-enacted over and over again in each and every life. There is always the hope of being restored to God, always the promise that human nature will be brought to its true fulfillment. God has never ceased to work for the redemption of his people.

Sin, like our creation, has its social as well as its personal side. It is as hard for a society as it is for an individual to cultivate a life of righteousness. War, discrimination, injustice to minorities, lack of concern for the weak and unprotected, unbridled national power—all these and more are the marks of sin in the life of society. And every member of society is involved in responsibility for these "sins" of society. No amount of hiding our heads in the sand can shut them out.

It is common when talking about a social problem like teen-age crime and violence to seek to put the blame on a particular group of people. We blame the teen-agers, or their parents, or the school system, or the publishers of comic books, or the producers of movies and television shows. We seek to find a single cause as explanation for a problem that has many causes. And we neglect to include ourselves as a part of the reason for what we label "juvenile delinquency." We forget that we share in maintaining the illusion that power and violence rule the world, that all that glitters is desirable, that things can take the place of love and concern. Our efforts to achieve personal righteousness are hollow and empty, if they seek to deny that we share in a Kingdom of Evil as well as in the Kingdom of God.

READING OURSELVES INTO THE BIBLE

Over and over we have found that the point of view of the Bible differs from what we have been accustomed to call the "Christian" point of view. The Bible knows no sharp distinction between the personal and the social, between the physical and the spiritual, between the secular and the sacred. Where we usually speak of "sins," the Bible is interested in sin itself. Instead of trying to discover the point of view of the Bible, we have been taught to read ourselves into the Bible. Nowhere do we do this more blatantly than when we try to read back into the stories and teachings of the Bible our modern emphasis on the individual and the value of personality.

How many of us believe—and have been taught to believe—that the Old Testament is a story of great religious personalities and their individual religious experiences. So, Abraham becomes for us a man of great faith who, because of his experience with the God Yahweh, leaves Ur and sets out for the West like an earlier-day Brigham Young. Moses becomes a heroic leader who, because of his experiences with the same Yahweh, leads the Hebrews out of Egypt and through the desert, stopping en route at Mount Sinai, where with God's help, he writes out the Declaration of Independence (Ten Commandments) and Constitution (Book of the Law) for the new nation of Israel. Isaiah is thought of as a young man who, after a searing personal experience with Yahweh in the Temple, serves as chaplain and spiritual advisor to the kings of Judah, while writing a book of prophecies about Jesus.

Such a reading of the Bible is as mistaken as thinking of Jesus in a double-breasted suit or the apostle Paul dictating his letters to a recording machine. It is reading ourselves into the Bible. Here is one of the central reasons why we have failed to see the Bible's relevance for social action. We have brought to the Bible a view of man that did not become a part of man's thinking until the time of the Renaissance, some fourteen centuries after Christ. To this we have added ideas of absolute personal freedom and of society as a collection of individuals—ideas that were current in France and England in the eighteenth century, but which were quite foreign to Palestine in the first century. We are tempted to read ourselves and our point of view into the Bible, to read it as a book completely about man as an individual. But when we try to understand the Bible's point of view, to read *about* ourselves in the Bible, we discover that the Bible knows man both as an individual and as a member of society.

THE BIBLE IS A SOCIAL BOOK

The Bible is a social book, a book that always speaks about man and his God—and his neighbor. In the epic of Israel in the Old Testament, we have the history of God's relations with a people, not with persons; with a society, not with individuals. For the Hebrews, there was no line of division between a man and his society; they were part of the same whole. Their way of looking at their world was in its simple way very much like the complicated, scientific way of modern sociology and social psychology. They believed that what a man did involved his whole society and that what a society did involved every one of its members. This fact can be seen quite clearly in God's promise to Abraham:

> "I will make of you a great nation, and I will bless you, and make your name great, so that you will be a blessing. I will bless those who bless you, and him who curses you I will curse; and by you all the families of the earth will bless themselves" (Gen. 12:2-3).

Although God spoke to Abraham, the descendants of Abraham understood that this promise involved not only this one man, but his whole family—both relations and descendants. The "name" of a man for the Hebrews lived through his children and their children. Therefore, when God promised Abraham that his "name" would be great, he meant that he would be remembered and that the influence of his family would continue after his death. More than this, "Abraham" does not mean merely the patriarch, or the patriarch and his immediate family; "Abraham" means also the twelve tribes of Israel, the whole society formed by the promise. So, the important part of the promise to Abraham was not what it meant for him personally, but what it meant for the group to which he belonged. He, like the rest of the Hebrews, did not think of himself as a person without thinking also of the fact that he belonged to a society.

This same social consciousness is found at other turning points in the history of Israel. When the Covenant is made at Sinai, it is not a covenant between God and Moses but between God and the people of Israel (Ex. 24:3-8). Moses is only the intermediary; God is the founder of Israel. The Ten Commandments show how closely personal identity and the sense of belonging to a society were joined in Hebrew thinking. Each commandment is in the personal form, "thou shalt" and "thou shalt not," addressed to each member of society individually. Yet these commandments are also laws of the Covenant, given to the people of Israel as a whole and forming the basis of their Law. The major purpose of the Ten Commandments, as of all the laws found in Exodus, Leviticus, Numbers, and Deuteronomy, was the well-being of society as God had intended it, and to violate these laws was to sin against God, the Lord of the Covenant, as well as to break the laws of society. The person, God, and the neighbor are all involved in the Covenant at Sinai and the Ten Commandments.

No word in the whole Bible expresses the close connection between the person and his society so clearly as the word *shalom,* "peace." For the Hebrews this was the most desirable state of life. But peace for them did not have our negative modern definition, "freedom from civil disturbance or war." The root of the word *shalom* in the Semitic languages means "wholeness," "being intact." Peace, for them, was a harmony, an order that encompassed all society. Also, peace for the Hebrews had nothing to do with "peace of mind" or "inner peace"; these phrases are not found in the Old Testament. Peace, for them, was always found in relation to others and to their God. It was never primarily an individual matter.

When Jews departed from each other, they would say: *"Shalom.* Go in peace." In this they were wishing each other safety, health, happiness, harmony with men and with God. God often promises peace to his people in the Bible. The work of redemption itself can be described as the establishment of peace by reconciling the breach between God and man, and between man and man—that is, sin. Here is the consummation of all that the Bible hopes for—the person at peace with his God, at peace with his neighbor, at peace with himself. Here is the proper goal for our social action.

When we come to understand the Bible's point of view and make it our own, we shall no longer be reading ourselves into the Bible; instead, we shall read about ourselves in the Bible.

For Your Personal Meditation and Study

Mark 12:28-34. It has been said, "Religion is what a man does with his solitude." Would Jesus have agreed with this definition? Do you agree with it?

Genesis 1:26-31; 2:4-24. If God made man in his own "image," can we say that man was made for society from the very beginning? Is there any real difference between saying, "Man *is* a soul" and "Man *has* a soul"?

Genesis 12:1-3. God's promise, although addressed to Abraham, is meant for Israel. How do later events in the Bible show this?

Exodus 20:1-17. On what basis does the truth of the Ten Commandments rest? In what way do they speak to the whole society as well as to individuals?

Psalm 122. This is a typical passage in which the word *shalom* (peace) occurs. Does it mean "freedom from civil disturbance or war"? Does it mean "peace of mind" and "inner peace"?

For Thought and Discussion

1. Many say, "The Bible speaks only of spiritual things." Is the church loyal to the Bible's point of view when the church and its members try to speak and act on local, national, and international issues?

2. Do the sermons and church school lessons in our churches speak too much of our relation to God? Of our relation to our neighbor?

3. Are there some issues and problems with which the church and church people should not concern themselves?

4. List some of the ways in which all men are social beings.

5. What are some of the consequences of sin in our present world? Are we all responsible for them, or must we hold certain groups and individuals responsible?

6. The Ten Commandments were the laws of God's covenant with Israel. How do they apply to people living in the modern world?

7. Some say, "Jesus introduced the concept of the individual into the world." Do you agree?

8. What is the basis of Christian social action?

9. What are the marks of *shalom* (peace) in today's life? Should we look for them only inside the churches or outside them as well?

2

THE WHOLE WORLD IN HIS HAND

"HE'S GOT THE WHOLE WORLD in his hand." This is the faith of the familiar spiritual. It is also the faith of the Bible. Our God is a *living* God, a God who *acts*. So Joshua could call the people of Israel together before they crossed over Jordan into the Promised Land and say:

> "Come hither, and hear the words of the Lord your God....
> Hereby you shall know that *the living God* is among you . . ."
> (Josh. 3:9-10).

This is the living God, the God of action who judges and redeems mankind, the God who moves on the scene of human history.

Few have stated that God is the Lord of history with the forcefulness of the prophet Jeremiah. His life and writings, as summed up for us in the Old Testament book bearing his name, restate the experience of Israel with the Lord God. Jeremiah catches up much that was said by the earlier prophets, while adding to them the stamp of his own age and its dealings with God. In a turbulent time, he could say that God truly has "the whole world in his hand."

A TIME OF TROUBLE AND CHANGE

Jeremiah lived through one of the most tumultuous periods in Israel's history. During his adult life he saw at least five kings sit upon the throne of David, two of them for less than a year. He saw the great Assyrian Empire, ruler of the ancient world, crumble and give way to the rising power of Babylon. The Northern Kingdom, Israel, already had gone into exile, and Jeremiah lived to see the first group of exiles go to Babylon and then the final fall of Jerusalem in 587 B.C. His experience was no less confused than that of a citizen of one of the Eastern European countries since the time of the first World War, or of a person who has lived in one of the new nations of Asia or the Middle East as it has struggled to be born.

We are accustomed to thinking of a world divided between two great powers, the United States and the Soviet Union. The international power situation in the time of Jeremiah was not much different. As in most of the history of ancient Israel, the Eastern world was divided between the empires of Mesopotamia and the Nile Valley. In Jeremiah's time, first Assyria and then Babylonia threatened Judah from bases on the Tigris and Euphrates Rivers to the East; while to the south the empire of Egypt sought to resist the spread of foreign influence among its neighbors. For small nations like Judah, caught between the hammer of Babylonia and the anvil of Egypt, there was no question of "neutralism." They had to choose sides—and be willing to take the consequences when the side they chose lost its power to defend them and sacrificed them to their enemy.

Judah in the time of Jeremiah had its share of domestic troubles as well. The king in his capital at Jerusalem was constantly receiving contradictory advice on foreign policy from his advisors, the "princes." Some were pro-Egypt, while others were first pro-Assyria and then later pro-Babylonia. The nation, therefore, steered an uneasy, vacillating course, depending on which set of advisors was able to get the ear of the king.

In addition, the religious life of the nation was in a state of turmoil. The worship of the nation centered in the Temple at Jerusalem, with its priests and prophets and scribes of the Law. But out on the land the people still made their sacrifices to the *baalim,* the nature gods of the Canaanites, and in the cities the sophisticates were performing the rites of Astarte, the Assyrian Queen of Heaven. If there was a question as to which great international power was to decide the destiny of Judah, there was also a question of which God or gods would have the most influence over the future.

Trouble and change were the lifetime heritage of Jeremiah's generation. Within Judah many of the most disturbing changes were the result of a steady transition from an agrarian society to a commercial, urban society. With the rise of commerce and trade, there arose also a commercial, trading class that had no respect for the older tribal traditions of family property. A new society based on money and the acquisition of personal property was being formed, and with it came a complex urban culture that scorned the older traditions and worked overtime to assimilate foreign ways. A generation like ours, that is seeing the world's peasants separated from the land by mass farming methods and the spread of industry to even the most underdeveloped areas, should be able to understand the widespread uncertainty that pervaded the life of Judah in the time of Jeremiah.

To Pluck Up and to Break Down . . . to Build and to Plant

The word of the Lord came to Jeremiah early in his life, but the terms of his call show the pattern of all the acts and messages of his ministry:

> "Before I formed you in the womb I knew you,
> and before you were born I consecrated you;
> I appointed you a prophet to the nations" (Jer. 1:5).

God's call to Jeremiah set him immediately in the middle of the history of his time. He was to be a prophet to "the nations"; i.e., a prophet not only to Judah, but also to all the rest of the inhabited world. God's jurisdiction did not end at the borders of the nation of Judah; it extended as far as the world he had created.

God placed Jeremiah in the place where he sat, "over nations and over kingdoms," so that he could proclaim to others the work of God in the world:

> "See, I have set you this day over nations and over kingdoms,
>   to pluck up and to break down,
>   to destroy and to overthrow,
>   to build and to plant" (Jer. 1:10).

Some people can see the work of God only in that which is creative, positive, and affirming. But Jeremiah, through the word of God placed in his mouth by the hand of God, knew that the very chaos and decay that caused some to doubt the power of ancient Israel's God was really a sign of God's power at work in the midst of human history.

In a time of trouble and change, many see their only hope to lie in holding on to what is old or in returning to former ways. They do not realize that some good must be sacrificed, some of what was old must be destroyed, if the new is to take its place. It is necessary "to pluck up and to break down, to destroy and to overthrow." After the leaders of his people had gone into exile in Babylon, Jeremiah felt deeply the fact that an age had come to an end and would never return. He could say:

> "Thus says the Lord:
> 'A voice is heard in Ramah,
>   lamentation and bitter weeping.
> Rachel is weeping for her children;
>   she refuses to be comforted for her children,
>   because they are not'" (Jer. 31:15).

Rachel, the wife of Jacob (Israel), was weeping inconsolably because of the exile of the two tribes named after her two children, Judah (Joseph) and Benjamin. Only in books about Utopia and in the imaginations of people who have lost touch with reality are born hopes that change will come painlessly and without loss and destruction. Jeremiah knew that this was a part of God's dealing with his world.

Yet the person who is a pessimist about human history finds as little comfort in Jeremiah's commission as does the cheery optimist. For God's work is creative as well as destructive, positive as well as negative, affirming as well as denying. Jeremiah was called "to build and to plant," as well as "to pluck up and to break down." A practical demonstration of this can be seen in the letter which he wrote to the first group of exiles taken to Babylon from Jerusalem and Judah:

> "Build houses and live in them; plant gardens and eat their produce. Take wives and have sons and daughters; . . . multiply there, and do not decrease" (Jer. 29:5-6).

Even in the midst of a difficult situation, God is deeply concerned for the welfare of mankind. He calls on men to build and to plant.

Here is a task to test the faith of us all. We know that "new occasions teach new duties, time makes ancient good uncouth." Yet we usually are unwilling to take part in any activity that we do not feel to be "creative" and "progressive." Jeremiah should teach us that there are times when to do the work of God means to have a part in plucking up, breaking down, destroying and overthrowing an old order. Our own American forebears reached the point where it was necessary to destroy their colonial relationship with Great Britain. All over the world today, new nations are arising out of the rubble of old arrangements. Those who see only the old and think of it as being the only good, call those who advocate the new "wreckers" and "destroyers." But we as Christians must be willing to bear the stigma of this name when the occasion demands it.

God also calls on men to build and to plant. And it takes every bit of our faith and understanding to know when the times call for this. God calls on men to "build" by every ability of critical analysis and understanding, of organization and technical skill, of personal and social discipline. Before us in the world today are monumental social tasks that call for all our best efforts. Yet God also calls for men to recognize that he is working too. They must be willing to "plant" and to see the tiny seed, which they cultivate and water, make its real growth, not by their efforts, but by the working of God. There comes a point at which our efforts can do no more, and we must be willing to allow the seed to grow. By all means, let us build; but let us also plant.

A FAITHLESS NATION

Jeremiah, like Isaiah and Hosea before him, declared that Israel, intended by God to be a righteous nation "holy to the Lord," had rebelled against God and had been unfaithful. Although he and his generation may have idealized the faithfulness of the Hebrew people in the wilderness, they were quite sure that God expected that the people who had made their covenant with him at Sinai would continue to be faithful to him. God desires a "holy" nation; not a nation faithful only in the keeping of religious observances, but a nation that lives its whole life in acknowledgment of God's rule over life.

But what God expected and what he got were two different things. What the sin of Israel was is set forth clearly in this important statement:

> ". . . my people have committed two evils:
>   they have forsaken me,
>   the fountain of living waters,
>   and hewed out cisterns for themselves,
>   broken cisterns,
>   that can hold no water" (Jer. 2:13).

God is the source of human life, "the fountain of living waters" or spring from which all blessings flow. But the people of Israel had forsaken the Lord of the world and had erected a false God for themselves; they had been satisfied with "broken cisterns" that could hold no water.

Some may say that this could be the sin of Israel only, because only Israel had been specially called by God to be "a kingdom of priests and a holy nation" (Ex. 19:6). Yet, covenant or no covenant, all the nations of the earth, including our own, have been created by God and are under his rule. "The fountain of living waters" still flows in our own time, but faithless men and nations are still hewing out "broken cisterns." Nationalism, racism, class exclusivism, colonialism, scientism, materialism—all these have their devotees and all these have their tragic results in our own time. Like Israel, many of those who give lip service to the Lord God and point to their long religious pedigree, are in reality worshiping at the altars of the false gods of this age.

GOD REQUIRES JUSTICE

Everywhere Jeremiah looked in the society of his day, he saw the results of faithlessness in the lives of the people.

> "Run to and fro through the streets of Jerusalem,
>   look and take note!
>   Search her squares to see
>   if you can find a man,
>   one who does justice
>   and seeks truth;
>   that I may pardon her" (Jer. 5:1).

Like the earlier prophets (cf. Micah 6:8), Jeremiah knew that God required justice and fair dealing between man and man. This was one of the marks of a "holy nation."

But wherever he looked he found injustice. Among the "poor," the common people, he found men swearing falsely and dealing unjustly with each other (Jer. 5:2-4). The "great," the leaders of society, were no better:

> "They lurk like fowlers lying in wait.
>   They set a trap;
>   they catch men.
>   Like a basket full of birds,
>   their houses are full of treachery;
>   therefore they have become great and rich,
>   they have grown fat and sleek.
>   They know no bounds in deeds of wickedness;
>   they judge not with justice
>   the cause of the fatherless, to make it prosper,
>   and they do not defend the rights of the needy"
>   (Jer. 5:26-28).

Poor and great, low and high—all shared in the injustice.

The civil and religious leaders were no better. Jeremiah condemned King Jehoiakim for building his palace with unjust taxes and neglecting to judge the cause of the poor and needy as his father, King Josiah, had done (Jer. 22:13-19). And the prophet was threatened with death when he criticized the priests by calling the Temple a "den of robbers" (Jer., chap. 26; see also chap. 7). As for the other prophets:

> "They have healed the wound of my people lightly,
>   saying, 'Peace, peace,'
>   when there is no peace" (Jer. 6:14).

Thinking here of "peace" as *shalom,* we can understand that they were saying, "All's well," when there was no wholeness or well-being in the nation.

> "For from the least to the greatest of them.
>   every one is greedy for unjust gain:
> and from prophet to priest,
>   every one deals falsely" (Jer. 6:13).

This picture of an unjust nation is merciless in its completeness, and brings to mind the words of Paul, "All have sinned and fall short of the glory of God."

The heart of the corruption of society in Judah was its faithlessness, the "broken cisterns" it had substituted for the living God.

> "They have spoken falsely of the Lord,
>   and have said, 'He will do nothing;
> no evil will come upon us,
>   nor shall we see sword or famine'" (Jer. 5:12).

Jeremiah's contemporaries were denying that God could act in history or do anything about the world that he had made. Here is an aspect of social action that many forget. When men deny God an active part in the life of the world, they are not likely to see the necessity for justice and fair dealing among men. "Whatever is, is right" becomes the motto of their lives. But when men see God at work in the lives of men and acknowledge that he rules over the world, their sense of the necessity for love and justice is increased.

THE LIVING GOD

"Arise, and go down to the potter's house" (Jer. 18:2). Thus spoke the living God to Jeremiah. On going to the potter's house, the prophet discovered him working at his wheel. When the vessel he was making out of the soft clay was spoiled in his hand, the potter did not throw it away, for the clay was still usable. Instead, "he reworked it into another vessel, as it seemed good to the potter to do." The Lord then said to Jeremiah:

"O house of Israel, can I not do with you as this potter has done? . . . Behold, like the clay in the potter's hand, so are you in my hand, O house of Israel" (Jer. 18:6).

A living God who is active in history can mold that history and change it as easily as the potter does the soft clay.

To believe in a living God is not the same as that rigid determinism which says: "God has a plan for every person and every nation. He will carry out that plan in every detail in spite of what we may do." Despite the potter's plan and intention, some vessels are spoiled; the clay does not take the form it should. So it is with God and man. God's immediate plan and intention—though not his ultimate will—can be affected by what men and nations do. No clearer example of this can be found in modern history than the beginning of our present time of troubles in the explosion of World War I in 1914. The political, economic, social, and military historians have all pored over the records of the events that led up to the assassination of Archduke Francis Ferdinand at Sarajevo. The nearly unanimous verdict is that the war could rather easily have been avoided if there had been more skilled leaders at the helm in Europe. No one really wanted the war or expected it to be as shattering to the order of Europe as it proved to be. But the clay was weak, and the Almighty's intention of peace was foiled by the weakness of men and of nations.

To believe in this kind of God does not mean, on the other hand, that the course of history is entirely a matter of human determination. The life of men and of nations is not decided completely by human wills. History is acted out not only among men; it is acted out also between men and God. The clay does not take form of itself; it is molded by the potter, even when the vessel does not turn out well. So also with God and man. Here again our recent history provides a vivid example in the rise of Adolf Hitler. Various political, economic, social, and psychological reasons have been given for his coming to power in Germany and the subsequent course of conquest that carried a whole continent down to ruin. No explanation has proved as satisfactory as the one given by the theologians who have called the source of Hitler's power "demonic," and have seen in him a judgment on the Western world. The Austrian painter and the Assyrian conqueror can both be the rod of God's anger and chastisement.

History is an interaction between men and their God. On the plane of human events, it is easy to think of history as involving only men and nations. But the eye of faith discerns that history, in fact, involves men and nations *and* the living God, a God who can both "pluck up and break down and destroy" and "build and plant."

> "If at any time I declare concerning a nation or a kingdom, that I will pluck up and break down and destroy it, and if that nation, concerning which I have spoken, turns from its evil, I will repent of the evil that I intended to do to it. And if at any time I declare concerning a nation or a kingdom that I will build and plant it, and if it does evil in my sight, not listening to my voice, then I will repent of the good which I had intended to do to it" (Jer. 18:7-10).

The living God could say this to the prophet in the potter's house concerning Judah, but the same alternatives are open to men and to nations in our day.

GOD OF THE NATIONS

"Make yourself thongs and yoke-bars, and put them on your neck," said the living God to Jeremiah (Jer. 27:2). Like other prophets before him, who had made themselves flesh-and-blood symbols of their message, Jeremiah after hearing these words wore a wooden ox-yoke around his neck, so that all who saw him would know that the Lord wished them to obey Nebuchadnezzar, king of Babylon. This word of God had come to Jeremiah:

"It is I who by my great power and my outstretched arm have made the earth, with the men and animals that are on the earth, and I give it to whomever it seems right to me. Now I have given all these lands into the hand of Nebuchadnezzar, the king of Babylon, my servant, and I have given him also the beasts of the field to serve him. All the nations shall serve him and his son and his grandson, until the time of his own land comes; then many nations and great kings shall make him their slave" (Jer. 27:5-7).

God was not only the God of Israel, but also the God of the nations, the God who could make even the despot Nebuchadnezzar serve his purposes.

To act and to speak in the time of King Zedekiah in such a manner as Jeremiah had done meant almost to commit treason. The king was surrounded by pro-Egyptian advisors who were urging him to depend on Egypt for protection and to join the kings of the neighboring small countries in revolt against Nebuchadnezzar, who already had besieged Jerusalem once and carried away captives and tribute. While they were counseling revolt, and while other prophets were saying that such revolt was the way to peace, Jeremiah was urging submission to Babylon as the only alternative to destruction. One of the optimistic prophets was Hananiah, who came to Jeremiah and broke the wooden yoke he wore around his neck, saying, "Thus says the Lord: Even so will I break the yoke of Nebuchadnezzar king of Babylon from the neck of all nations within two years" (Jer. 28:11). Jeremiah went his way, but later he heard from God that God had put "upon the neck of all these nations an iron yoke of servitude to Nebuchadnezzar, king of Babylon, and they shall serve him" (Jer. 28:14).

Although it is easy to see the political difference between

Jeremiah and Hananiah (one was pro-Babylon, the other pro-Egypt), it is not so easy to recognize that at the heart of their difference lay a fundamental disagreement about the nature of God. Where Hananiah thought of God basically as the God of Israel, a God who wanted nothing but peace for his chosen people and who would always favor them above all other nations, Jeremiah recognized that God was the God of the nations—of Egypt and Babylon, of Edom, Moab, Ammon, Tyre, and Sidon, as well as of Israel. Jeremiah saw God moving not only in the affairs of the "holy nation" Israel, but also in the affairs of *all* nations.

In an age that has coined the word "globaloney" and in a country where many find it hard to conceive that the full life is possible anywhere else on the face of the earth, we need to remember that God is the God of the nations. The Soviet Union and the sub-continent of China living by the teachings of Marx, the Arab nations and the new democracies of Southeast Asia which are driven by the passions of nationalism and anti-colonialism, the old countries of the West, the submerged and dependent peoples of all continents—every one of them has as full a place in God's purpose as the colossus that is America. In this respect it is well for Christians not to be impatient with a body like the General Assembly of the United Nations, which can never reach quick and unanimous agreement, but must always allow full and free interplay among its members, large and small. God has no particular "chosen nation" or "chosen bloc," but he can use all nations in the working out of his will.

Also, in an age which has discovered that man in society has other loyalties that often can supersede his loyalty to country—loyalty to class, to race, to caste, to cultural faith— we need to remember that God is the God of the nations. Socialism, Marxism, and other proletarian movements have

made much of the role of the working class and have called
it the "wave of the future," whereas capitalism and liberal
democracy have made much of the role of the middle class.
Yet if God is God of the nations, he may give dominance
now to one and now to the other, but will never cease to
be the God of both. So also with the conflict between the
fair and the dark-skinned peoples of the world, between the
educated and the ignorant, between the skilled and the un-
skilled, and between the various philosophies and world-
views current in our time. The God

> ". . . who sits above the circle of the earth,
>   and its inhabitants are like grasshoppers;
> who stretches out the heavens like a curtain,
>   and spreads them like a tent to dwell in;
> who brings princes to nought,
>   and makes the rulers of the earth as nothing"
> (Isa. 40:21-23)

is a God who rules them all and cares for them all.

A NEW COVENANT

Jeremiah knew God to have power over the nations, but
he also worshiped the Lord as "the God of Abraham and
Isaac and Jacob," as the Lord of the Covenant who had
chosen Israel for a special mission to the rest of the world.
So great was Jeremiah's love for Israel and the Covenant
that he looked forward to the time when Israel would no
longer be unfaithful and the Covenant would no longer
be broken.

> "Behold, the days are coming, says the Lord, when I will
> make a new covenant with the house of Israel and the house
> of Judah, not like the covenant which I made with their
> fathers when I took them by the hand to bring them out of
> the land of Egypt, my covenant which they broke, though I
> was their husband, says the Lord. But this is the covenant
> which I will make with the house of Israel after those days,

says the Lord: I will put my law within them, and I will write it upon their hearts; and I will be their God, and they shall be my people. And no longer shall each man teach his neighbor and each his brother, saying, 'Know the Lord,' for they shall all know me, from the least of them to the greatest, says the Lord; for I will forgive their iniquity, and I will remember their sin no more" (Jer. 31:31-34).

The God who made covenant with Abraham and Moses would make a "new covenant" with his people Israel.

The major difference between this new covenant and the first covenant that was promised to Abraham and sealed at Sinai is that under the new covenant all would obey the Lord because his law would be written upon their hearts. There are some who understand this to mean that whereas the old covenant was between God and the nation Israel, the new covenant would be directly between God and the individual. This misreads the words of the prophet. The new covenant, like the old, involves all the children of Abraham ("the house of Israel and the house of Judah"); the new covenant, like the old, is designed for the welfare of society as well as for the welfare of the individual. The new covenant means that the people who had made for themselves "broken cisterns that can hold no water" would return to the "fountain of living waters," the Lord of their life.

Jeremiah was not a cynic; he was not one of the company who believed mankind to be past hope of recovery. If he had looked only at the change and decay in the world around him, if he had considered only the faithlessness and injustice in the life of Judah, he would soon have given up. But Jeremiah believed also in a God who had "the whole world in his hand," he believed in a God who could forgive iniquity and remember sin no more. Therefore, Jeremiah could look forward to the New Covenant in which all that had been promised to Israel in the Old Covenant would be fulfilled. We know now that his hopes were not vain, for we live in that age of the New Covenant which now knows the Lord as Father and Redeemer.

For Your Personal Meditation and Study

Jeremiah 1:4-10. Compare the call of Jeremiah with that of Isaiah (Isa. 6:13). Is Jeremiah unique among the prophets in being "set over nations and over kingdoms" both "to pluck up and to break down" and "to build and to plant"?

Jeremiah 2:1-13. God is described in many ways in the Bible. What does the title "the fountain of living waters" suggest to you? Did Israel willingly exchange this fountain for its "broken cisterns"?

Jeremiah 5:1-17, 20-31; 6:13-15. Jeremiah found his society full of corruption and injustice "from the least to the greatest." Is he unfair in condemning the poor who are only following the example of their rulers? Are the poor to be excused because of their poverty?

Jeremiah 18:1-12. Some, reading this passage, emphasize the fact that the potter (God) is in complete control of the clay. Others say Jeremiah's intention is to show that even though a vessel may be spoiled, the potter (God) can make another out of it. With which opinion do you agree? Does it change your idea of God?

Jeremiah 28:1-14; 29:1-9. Jeremiah was convinced that God would continue the rule of Nebuchadnezzar over Judah. Would you say on the basis of these two incidents that he was or was not a prophet of "peace" (*shalom*)?

Jeremiah 31:31-34. What did the New Covenant mean to Jeremiah and the people who heard him? What does it mean to us today?

For Thought and Discussion

1. We often speak of God as upholding "the things that are eternal." Does God also reveal himself in trouble and change?

2. On political and social issues over which there is sharp disagreement, can we assume that God never favors one side over against the other?

3. Can you think of a social issue in which change takes place without losing or sacrificing some values? Must there always be some plucking up and breaking down?

4. Can Christians take part in a cause which has only a negative purpose?

5. How are we to distinguish between situations in which we are called to "build" by our own efforts and situations in which we should "plant" and allow to grow by God's efforts?

6. Can you name some "broken cisterns" which modern men have substituted for the living God? Is our country as shot through with faithlessness and injustice as was Jeremiah's?

7. "History is an interaction between men and their God." Do you agree with this statement? Does it diminish the omnipotence of God or the free will of man?

8. We say that God is "God of the nations." Does this mean that he has power over them as political and social units or only over their citizens as individuals?

9. If the New Covenant is inward and written upon men's hearts, should we have any concern for legislation and other external controls?

3

KING OF KINGS AND LORD OF LORDS

IN ALMOST EVERY COMMUNITY, at the Christmas or Easter season, one has an opportunity to hear the glorious words and music of the "Hallelujah Chorus" from Handel's *Messiah:*

> "The kingdom of this world is become
>   The kingdom of our Lord, and of his Christ;
> And he shall reign for ever and ever,
>   King of Kings and Lord of Lords.
> Hallelujah! Hallelujah! Hallelujah!"

The music, sung by a mighty chorus supported by organ and orchestra, is enough to carry away the senses. But the words are even more marvelous than the music: "He [Christ] shall reign for ever and ever, King of Kings and Lord of Lords."

These words are derived, of course, from Revelation 11: 15. Yet the whole of the New Testament makes as a statement of everyday fact the very same affirmation that the "Hallelujah Chorus" expresses in ineffable harmonies. We live in a new age; the world already has changed and already has become the kingdom of our God. Christ rules this world and is its Lord. To be sure, the members of the Church still pray as Christ has taught them:

> "Thy kingdom come,
>   Thy will be done,
>   On earth as it is in heaven."

We must wait for the coming of the kingdom; but also we know its reality in our midst. It is difficult to say which way of expressing the present state of the world is harder for us to understand, the lofty statement in song and poetry or the constantly repeated statement of fact. However, both agree on who Jesus of Nazareth is today; he is King of kings, he is Lord of lords.

FULFILLED, NOT ABOLISHED

There are those who would like to place the new state of the world since the coming of Christ in absolute opposition to all that had been before. They do not realize that the New Testament must be understood in relation to the Old Testament, that the New Covenant presupposes the Old Covenant. (The word "Testament" and the word "Covenant" are practically interchangeable.) Although God created "something new" in sending his Son into the world, he did not do this wholly outside the framework of what had gone before.

Our Lord Jesus himself was aware of the continuity of his ministry with the previous history of Israel. When he stood up to read in the synagogue at Nazareth and to proclaim the beginning of his mission, he read from the book of the prophet Isaiah the remarkable words which describe the mission of the Servant of the Lord, the Anointed One (Messiah), who was to be the Redeemer and Savior of his people.

> "The Spirit of the Lord is upon me,
>   because he has anointed me to preach good news to the poor.
>   He has sent me to proclaim release to the captives
>   and recovering of sight to the blind,
>   to set at liberty those who are oppressed,
>   to proclaim the acceptable year of the Lord" (Luke 4:18-19;
>   see also Isa. 61:1-2).

After he had finished reading and had sat down, Jesus said to the people, "Today this scripture has been fulfilled in your hearing."

This same sense of the heritage of Israel expresses itself in one of the key passages of the Sermon on the Mount (Matt., chaps. 5-7). When introducing his own stricter interpretation of the Law, an interpretation which considers a person's intentions and motives to be as significant as his actions, Jesus said:

> "Think not that I have come to abolish the law and the prophets; I have come not to abolish them but to fulfill them" (Matt. 5:17).

The older laws of the covenant-community of Israel were not being replaced. Instead, the New Covenant predicted by Jeremiah was being brought into being.

The important word in both of these statements is the word, "fulfill" (the Greek verb is *plēroō*). Jesus came to "fulfill" all that God had done before through Israel, not to abolish it. The community of the covenant, instead of passing away, is now extended to include all the peoples of the nations. The Law of Israel, expressed in the Ten Commandments, is now known to be fundamental for all human life. The hopes of the prophets for deliverance and a New Covenant are now shown to be fact. In short, all that had been known and hoped for under the Old Covenant is made real and brought to fullness in the New Covenant.

It has been popular in Protestant churches to say that the New Testament, in contrast to the Old, is individualistic, that it places primary emphasis on the responsibility of the individual. This has led some to disregard the Old Testament completely, considering it to be a work offering no assistance or insight to the Christian. However, a careful reading of both Testaments will show that the Bible, from Genesis to Revelation, always speaks of man in society. The

Bible recognizes that man is both an individual and a member of society.

THE NEWNESS OF THE GOSPEL

The good news of Jesus' coming (i.e., the gospel) speaks of the Old Covenant as "fulfilled" in the New; but it also declares that God created "something new" in Jesus Christ. In one of the earliest Christian sermons, that delivered by Peter at the Beautiful Gate of the Temple, we can catch this mixture of old and new:

> "The God of Abraham and of Isaac and of Jacob, the God of our fathers, glorified his servant Jesus, whom you delivered up and denied in the presence of Pilate, when he had decided to release him. But you denied the Holy and Righteous One, and asked for a murderer to be granted to you, and killed the Author of life, whom God raised from the dead. To this we are witnesses. . . . And now, brethren, I know that you acted in ignorance, as did also your rulers. But what God foretold by the mouth of all the prophets, that his Christ should suffer, he thus fulfilled. Repent, therefore, and turn again, that your sins may be blotted out, that times of refreshing may come from the presence of the Lord, and that he may send the Christ appointed for you, Jesus, whom heaven must receive until the time for establishing all that God spoke by the mouth of his holy prophets from of old" (Acts 3:13-15, 17-21).

We remember the Old Covenant when we read of "the God of Abraham and of Isaac and of Jacob, the God of our fathers," and also when we hear Jesus described as God's "servant," a designation that recalls the descriptions of the Messiah as the "Servant of the Lord" in Isaiah, chaps. 52-53. But we recognize that we are in the presence of "something new" when Peter declares Jesus to be "the Author of Life, whom God raised from the dead", and when the people are urged to repent "that your sins may be blotted out."

That which has been from of old is "fulfilled," but the gospel also speaks of a new fact.

For the apostles and for all who heard their gospel, the resurrection was the great sign of this new fact. This is made clear in the final words of Peter's sermon at Pentecost:

> "Let all the house of Israel therefore know assuredly that God has made him both Lord and Christ, this Jesus whom you crucified" (Acts 2:36).

By the resurrection, the disciples knew that Jesus had gained a position which the Jewish faith had always reserved for the Lord God himself. Jesus is both "Lord" and "Christ"— titles that fall on our ears with an easy familiarity because we are so used to repeating them, but titles that came with sudden new impact to the ears of the Jews who had gathered to learn what was taking place on that day.

God has made Jesus *Lord*. The word here translated "Lord" (*Adonai*) is the title which Jews reserved for God himself. To call Jesus "Lord" is to say that he shares the place of God as ruler of heaven and earth, that he now also holds "the whole world in his hand." Before Christ came, it was possible to think of God only as the God of Israel, "the God of Abraham and of Isaac and of Jacob." Now that Christ has come, we must also recognize God as "the Father of our Lord Jesus Christ." It is not enough for our faith and life as Christians to be grounded in the God of the Old Covenant; now they can be made fuller through the Christ of the New Covenant. God has given the world into Christ's hands, and now we must acknowledge him as our ruler.

God has also made Jesus the *Christ*. This was the title used by Jews for the Messiah, the promised King from the line of David who would come and rule over a restored Israel. (*Christos* in the Greek means "the anointed one" or king.) To say that Jesus is "the Christ" is to affirm that salvation is already here, that men must no longer look to the future for their redemption. For Jews who were looking for the consolation of Israel there was the constant hope of a "new age" when the good purposes of God for his creation and for his people would be fulfilled. Now that the Christ has come, we know that this new age has already begun. "The kingdom of the world has become the kingdom of our Lord and of his Christ" (Rev. 11:15).

THE DEPTH OF THE GOSPEL

There is a deeper dimension to the good news of the gospel; namely, that in Jesus Christ the gulf of sin has been crossed and man can be restored through divine forgiveness. This too was proclaimed by Peter at Pentecost:

> "Now when they heard this they were cut to the heart, and said to Peter and the rest of the apostles, 'Brethren, what shall we do?' And Peter said to them, 'Repent, and be baptized every one of you in the name of Jesus Christ for the forgiveness of your sins . . .'" (Acts 2:37-38).

Since Eden man has had to live his life with the consequences of sin. But in Jesus Christ, God has offered forgiveness by the gift of his own Son.

The story of Adam and Eve in the Garden testifies to the fact of sin in human life. But the life and death and resurrection of Jesus Christ testifies to the fact that God's good purpose for the human race has not been defeated. Paul gets to the heart of this profound dimension of the gospel story when he declares:

> "Therefore, if any one is in Christ, he is a new creation; the old has passed away, behold, the new has come. All this is from God, who through Christ reconciled us to himself . . . ; that is, God was in Christ reconciling the world to himself, not counting their trespasses against them, and entrusting to us the message of reconciliation. . . . We beseech you on be-

half of Christ, be reconciled to God. For our sake he made him to be sin who knew no sin, so that in him we might become the righteousness of God" (2 Cor. 5:17-21).

Here is a statement that is clear and direct: The gulf of sin which has always separated men from God has been crossed from God's side by Jesus Christ (him "who knew no sin") and we are brought back ("reconciled") to God. By repenting of our sins and believing in what God has done in Jesus Christ, we too can become new.

Anyone who has struggled with the stubbornness of his own sin and realized that "I do not do the good I want, but the evil I do not want is what I do" (Rom. 7:19); anyone who has felt the extent to which he lives apart from and at odds with his fellow men; anyone who has finally been forced to acknowledge that he is a fugitive from God and a stranger in the universe—anyone, that is, who knows the depth of sin and its consequences, knows also that the clear and direct statement of God's reconciling love in Jesus Christ has depths that are beyond human knowledge or experience. One can only say that here is the heart of the Bible, as it is also the heart of the good news, the gospel. And here also is the heart of Christian social action.

WHAT GOD HAS DONE

We do not find the chief source of social action as Christians where many expect to find it. Some would have us look exclusively to the *example and teachings of Jesus,* as we find them recorded in the Gospels for our motive and guide. It is quite certain that Jesus thought of his ministry as ushering in the new age of the Kingdom of God. He himself lived the life of that new age and exhorted his disciples to recognize that it had come. But after his death and resurrection we do not find the apostles appealing very often to what Jesus had taught. They were more deeply motivated by what God had done through Jesus: "God was in Christ reconciling the world to himself. . . ." How Jesus lived and what he taught are very important to us, but we would do well to remember that he promised that "he who believes in me will also do the works that I do; and greater works than these will he do" (John 14:12). God's love made available through the cross of Christ is more precious than God's love as taught or lived by him.

Some others would have us look to *the example and exhortation of the apostles and early church* for our guide in social action. The life of the Jerusalem church as described in Acts 2:44-47 is often cited as a model of the perfect society. The various exhortations on problems of daily life which Paul placed at the end of his letters (for an example, see Rom., chaps. 12-15) are thought by many to be an adequate statement of the life God expects a Christian to lead. Here again it is important to know the way in which the Christians of the first century lived and taught, for they were the first to feel the immediate impact of the gospel. But we are Christians of the twentieth century, and many of the problems of the first century no longer concern us, while new problems of far greater complexity have arisen to test us. The reconciling love of God known in the middle of our own present situation is of far greater importance to us than the record of how others responded to that love in an earlier time.

So we are led back to the central fact of our faith, which must also be the basis of our action in society: what God has done and is doing in Jesus Christ. God's love has been shown to be real and all-powerful in the death and resurrection of Christ. What God has done, shows us that evil and sin and death cannot triumph over his love. Even more important, what God is doing brings that love as power and reality into the life of men. D. T. Niles, of Ceylon, has said it this way: "To live in a world where Jesus is risen is to live in a world where Jesus is Lord."[1] All our social action must take into account this central fact that Jesus is now King of kings and Lord of lords.

This may seem the height of irrelevance, for it does not start where the world is with all its problems and where we are, but rather starts with what God has done and is doing. Niles has a dialogue which explains in beautiful fashion why this is necessary:

> "We are concerned with schemes of practical reform to make this our present world a better world to live in. For many the claim of Christ that he is the way is the most compelling claim of all. But is he? Has he a vision of that better world?"
>
> "Yes, he has, and no man has ever conceived a grander ideal than his of the Kingdom of God operative on earth."
>
> "Has he a method and technique?"
>
> "He has, a method without compulsion or casuistry, the only method which up to date has achieved anything of lasting value."
>
> "Has he a plan?"
>
> "Yes, he has: first Galilee, then Jerusalem, then Gethsemane and Calvary, and finally Easter Morning."
>
> "But what about actual plans for us, the hard details of this campaign to make a better world?"
>
> "Christ's answer to that is simply 'first enlist.' Does that seem to be an evading of the issue? Nevertheless it is his answer. 'First enlist, and then you will receive orders. First befriend Me and then you will know My purpose. First follow Me and then you will learn My plans.'"
>
> "But Master Christ! How do I know that Thy way leads to that better world?"
>
> "You know because it is My way."[2]

This is where we must begin in Christian social action.

[1] From *That They May Have Life,* by D. T. Niles. Page 28. Copyright, 1951, by The Student Volunteer Movement for Christian Missions. Harper & Brothers, publishers. Used by permission.

[2] *Ibid.,* p. 29. Paragraphing slightly adapted.

SAVIOR OF THE WORLD

God acts first—and we act in response to his action; we act in consciousness of what he has done and is doing. But this does not mean that God's action in Jesus Christ was only intended for men as individuals. Our response to his action begins with our personal act of repentance and faith, but this does not mean that God is only acting through and for individuals. In plain fact, he acts through all the structures of society as well as of personality in performing his redemptive will.

The apostles and the early church were fully conscious of this fact. Their customary way of speaking about Christ was to say that he died "for *us*" or "for *our* sins." We are so accustomed to hearing the minister say, "Christ died for *you*" (individually), and to say ourselves, "Christ died for *me*," that we lose sight of the fact that Christ's work was for all men, for all human society.

This can be seen even more clearly when we look at the well-beloved summary of the gospel message in John 3:16:

> "For God so loved *the world* that he gave his only Son, that whoever believes in him should not perish but have eternal life. For God sent the Son into *the world*, not to condemn *the world*, but that *the world* might be saved through him" (John 3:16-17).

The key word here is "world" (*kosmos* in the Greek). It is the "world" that God loved, it is the "world" into which he sent his Son, it is the "world" that is saved. *Kosmos* meant to the Greeks the whole inhabited earth, all of human society. It was not the world in its geographical extent, the various countries on the globe; it was the world of men, of all men. To say that Christ is the Savior of the world is to say that he is the Savior of all men, the Savior of all human society.

Here is where much of our Christian social action has got off the track. Understanding that each person must accept for himself the salvation offered by God in Christ, many Christians have come to believe that salvation is completely individual. They have refused to acknowledge that since Christ is the Savior of the world, all of human society shares in his work of redemption. This, in turn, has led them to feel that social action is completely outside the commissioned task of the church.

Other Christians have recognized the necessity for social redemption, but have been convinced that the redemption of society is accomplished only through the redemption of individuals. This, too, limits Christ's saving action to the life of the individual and refuses to acknowledge the corporateness of human life, the close bond of society in which we all are gathered together.

Christian social action has an obligation to work through all the structures of society as well as those of human personality. God's work of redemption has occurred in the middle of the real world. Christ came as a Jew; he was born under a Roman government, lived in a particular age in the world's history. By coming in human form, he showed how important the life of man is to God. It is a queer distortion of faith in him that denies the importance of the life of this world and focusses only on the internal life of the believer or on the life of the world to come. If Christ is the Savior of the world, then the whole life of the world is within the scope of redemption. Our fellow men can be approached individually, but they can also be approached and deeply influenced through those structures of society of which they are a part and which form so large a part of their lives. The government under which they live, the associations to which they belong, the organizations which direct their work life, the media of communication to which they listen, the class or social group from which they take most of their views on life—all of these are part of the fabric of the world. It is the "world"—all of human life—for which Christ died. We fail to take Christ seriously when we limit the areas of life in which God's redemption can be found to be effective.

We offer men only part of the gospel—and we greatly limit our own ability to be ministers of that gospel—when we approach them one by one and speak of Christ only as their individual Savior. He is also "the Savior of the world"; he is Lord of every area of human life, that social life which presses in upon a man and influences his every action, as well as that personal life which proceeds out of his own consciousness and will. Christ is truly a "personal Savior," who redeems us not only in the solitude of our soul but also in the complex network of our life in society. My Christ is also the world's Christ.

THE BODY OF CHRIST

The Bible bears testimony to this corporateness of human life. After Christ's work was done, he left behind him not only the gospel, the message of the good news of God's salvation, but also the Church, the community or fellowship based upon his work. The Church is a new society created by the action of God as surely as was the old society of Israel. The new life of faith is not merely a life lived in solitary communion with God through Jesus Christ; it is a life lived in the new community of faith, the Church.

The New Testament has many ways of describing this new life in the new community, the Church. The Church is "the body of Christ," "the household of faith," the "family" of Christ, the "New Covenant," "the bride of Christ," "the assembly," "the Vine with its branches," "little flock," "synagogue," "fellowship" (*koinōnia* in the Greek), "church" (*ekklēsia* in the Greek, which may be literally translated "congregation of the faithful" or "those who have been called out"). None of these words speaks of solitude and personal isolation. Every one assumes corporate involvement in the life of a community.

The Church is the Body of Christ, and Paul's description of that Body makes clear how impossible it is to conceive of a man as being a Christian apart from belonging to the fellowship of the Church:

> "For just as the body is one and has many members and all the members of the body, though many are one body, so it is with Christ. For by one Spirit we were all baptized into one body—Jews or Greeks, slaves or free—and all were made to drink of one Spirit. For the body does not consist of one member but of many. . . . If one member suffers, all suffer together; if one member is honored, all rejoice together. Now you are the body of Christ and individually members of it" (1 Cor. 12:12-14, 26-27).

As Christians we all are members of the Body of Christ and must take our place in the life of the Church.

The mark of this new community is the gift of the Holy Spirit. Jesus told the disciples, "You shall receive power when the Holy Spirit has come upon you" (Acts 1:8); and the Holy Spirit came to them when they were assembled in fellowship, came to them as a group, not to particular individuals. Throughout the Book of Acts and the other books of the New Testament, the Holy Spirit is the Church-building, fellowship-forming power. The "gifts" of the Spirit described by Paul (see 1 Cor., chap. 12) are the various ministries of the Church. It is not surprising that the most common benediction used by Christians should pray thus: "The grace of the Lord Jesus Christ and the love of God and the fellowship of the Holy Spirit be with you all" (2 Cor. 13:14). The new life in Christ is a new life in the "fellowship" (*koinōnia*) of the Church and "the fellowship (*koinōnia*) of the Holy Spirit."

The Bible throughout bears witness to the corporateness of human life. From the creation of human society when the man and the woman were placed in the Garden down to the present time when we can know the new life in the Church, man has not been alone and cannot live his life unto himself. One of our present-day Bible scholars has written:

> "The biblical story must not be interpreted as the progressive emancipation of the individual, but instead as God's action in history to create a community in which the responsible individual finds his true being.[3]

The point of view of the Bible remains constant from Adam to Christ. Man always lives his life in relation both to God and to his neighbors. And the original life of fellowship which was broken by sin has been restored through Christ in the fellowship of the Church.

> "So then you are no longer strangers and sojourners, but you are fellow citizens with the saints and members of the household [family] of God, built upon the foundation of the apostles and prophets, Christ Jesus himself being the chief cornerstone, in whom the whole structure is joined together and grows into a holy temple in the Lord; in whom you also are built into it for a dwelling place of God in the Spirit" (Eph. 3:19-22).

For Your Personal Meditation and Study

Luke 4:16-21. Jesus says these words from Isaiah are "fulfilled." In what way are they "fulfilled"? Does he mean only that they have come true and are no longer important?

Matthew 5:17-20. "The law" contained the rules for

---

[3] From *The Biblical Doctrine of Man in Society,* by G. Ernest Wright. Published, 1954, by S. C. M. Press, London. U. S. agent, Alec R. Allenson, Inc., Naperville, Ill. Used by permission.

life under the Old Covenant made at Sinai, and "the prophets" bore witness to God's continuing work in history. When Jesus says that neither of these has been abolished but that both are fulfilled, what does he mean?

Acts 3:12-26. Jesus is called "the Author of life." What has he done to deserve this title? Jesus is called "the Christ." What do you understand this title to mean? Why does Peter call upon the people to repent?

2 Corinthians 5:16-21. If we all were originally made by God according to his purpose, why is there any need for "reconciliation"? Do you feel the need to be reconciled to God? Why did it take the death and resurrection of Christ to reconcile the world to God?

John 3:16-21. What has this word "world" meant to you in the past? Wherein does this passage gain new meaning when "world" is understood in its original meaning of all of human society?

1 Corinthians 12:4-27. What is "the body of Christ"? Notice the way in which the Holy Spirit plays a part in forming and moving the body of Christ. Compare this passage with Jesus' description of himself as the Vine (John 15:1-17).

Ephesians 2:11-22. Was the cross necessary to reconcile men to God and to each other? In the Old Testament, peace (*shalom*) meant the well-being of the whole community; does it mean the same here? Can we be "fellow citizens" and "members of the household [family]" if we live wholly to ourselves?

For Thought and Discussion

1. Is it a contradiction to say that God is the ruler of the universe and that Jesus Christ is "King of kings and Lord of lords"?

2. In what ways does the New Covenant introduced by Christ differ from the Old Covenant given to Israel at Sinai?

3. Why is it incorrect to say that the New Covenant is more individualistic than the Old Covenant?

4. Sin damages man's relation to God, his relation to his neighbors in society, and his own consciousness of himself. How does the forgiveness of sins in Jesus Christ set these areas of man's life to rights again?

5. If the work of Christ was "reconciliation," can we as Christians take part in any other activities except those which result in reconciliation? Is our main task that of bringing peace and harmony?

6. Do you agree that the chief source of Christian social action is not in the example and teachings of Jesus or in the life of the apostles and the early church, but rather in God's redemption of the world through Jesus Christ?

7. How is it possible to get from belief in salvation through Christ to the many problems of the world, such as war and peace, the conflict between labor and management, and prejudice and discrimination between the races?

8. What does it mean to say, "Jesus Christ is my personal Savior"?

9. What is the "world" in our present-day life?

10. Can we conceive of Christian faith without life in the Church?

11. Does the Church have certain jobs to perform in the world and certain areas where it has its place, or is the Church involved in all of human life with an unlimited responsibility?

4

THE GOSPEL OF ACTION

"But what are your churches doing about it?" This is a question frequently put to us as Christians whenever we start to talk with someone about the ills of the world or the social problems that disturb the life of our times and scar the lives of our fellow men. People seldom question our sincerity or the need for Christians to have an interest in social, political, and economic affairs; what they question is our inactivity, our failure to do anything about the problems we can see. In the eyes of the world, we might as well be singing this parody which someone has made of a familiar hymn:

> "Stand pat, O men of God.
> The world with problems great
> Has tasks unequal to your strength.
> Stand pat—and make them wait."

Inactivity, not action, seems to be what Christians too often contribute to the solution of the problems of the world.

Yet action is the keynote of the Bible story. From its first to its last book, the Bible tells of the action of God in history. He it was who delivered Israel from Egypt and formed the people into a nation through the covenant made at Sinai. He it was who spoke through the prophet Jeremiah to a world of change and decay. He it was who sent his own Son, Jesus Christ our Lord, to live and breathe and die in the world of the Caesars. And he it was who raised up

59

Jesus and continues to work with men for their redemption. The whole story of the Bible is one of action, the good news of God's action in history. The Bible should not be considered primarily as a book containing a catalog of principles that never change, or a code of laws that offers a comprehensive guide for life, or an analysis of social forces and powers that follow a never-varying pattern in human history. When we look at the Bible in this way, we miss the most important characteristic of its pages. What we have in the Bible is the record of the constant activity of the living God in the history of the world and in the lives of men.

DOERS OF THE WORD

"But be doers of the word, and not hearers only, deceiving yourselves" (James 1:22). We deceive ourselves in believing that we have a true faith, if we know what God has done and then, having listened to the record of his deeds, we talk about those deeds without acting ourselves. For God's action demands our action in response. When Israel entered into covenant with the Lord, she was expected to lead a life under the Commandments as his chosen people. When Jeremiah spoke for the Lord to the people of Judah, they were expected to respond by "returning" to God and repenting of their evil ways. When Jesus Christ came to give his life for the world, we all were asked to believe in him and to act henceforth as those who know God's redeeming work. To believe without acting, to be "hearers" and not "doers," is hypocrisy. And too much of the life of our churches is precisely that!

When a man becomes a Christian and joins one of our churches, he is asked to believe in what God has done. His confession of faith puts him on record as standing on the Lord's side. But every one of us is a whole man—we have not only souls and minds but also bodies. If we then are to love God with all our "heart and soul and mind *and strength*," our actual deeds are fully as important as our statement of faith. Yet very few of our churches ask much of us in the way of action, and what they do ask is usually in the sphere of our private morality, abstaining from swearing, drunkenness, sexual impurity, and the like. Our churches seldom ask us to examine the society of which we are a part, and they do not offer us much guidance in social matters or provide any channels for social action in the world.

This is in direct contradiction to the nature of the gospel. Jesus' own ministry consisted of *deeds* of love and mercy, not solely of words concerning God's love. The life of the early Church, which bore such an effective witness to what Christ had done in the world, was marked by sharing with each other and by service to those outside. The apostle Paul did not write a letter to any one of the churches without asking what its members were doing, as well as what they believed and said. The Lord Jesus himself has made it plain that discipleship must be in deed as well as in word: "By this my Father is glorified, that you bear much fruit, and so prove to be my disciples" (John 15:8).

THE KINGDOM IN THE MIDST OF YOU

The root of the Christian's failure to be active often is found in the notion that religion is a private matter between man and his God. The favorite proof text for this inadequate form of Christianity is Jesus' statement that "the kingdom of God is within you" (Luke 17:21, KJV). In the secret place of the soul, many say, is where a man meets God and where he must give answer to him. This is considered to be religion, while all questions of living in society lie in a separate area of ethics for which a person's faith provides the motivation and guidance. The truest work of God, according to this interpretation, is to be found within a man's soul.

Important as personal religious experience is to the life of faith, we must not be misled into believing that religion is merely a private matter. Newer translations of this favorite New Testament verse show that Jesus was not saying that the kingdom of God is a personal possession at all. The preposition formerly translated "within" actually means "in the midst," and the verse should be read thus: "Behold, the kingdom of God is *in the midst of you.*" The kingdom of God is right in the middle of human society, right in the middle of history. The Pharisees had asked Jesus when the kingdom was going to come, and his answer was that the kingdom of God had already come. We already are part of the kingdom of God; it lies in and around us.

What sort of kingdom did Jesus have in mind? If it surrounds us, then we are mistaken if we think of it only as a place (heaven) to which we shall go in the future. Furthermore, if it is already here, then we are mistaken if we continue to believe it is like the ideal society described by Plato in his *Republic,* which existed only as an ideal that would someday be brought into being. The kingdom of God about which Jesus taught, is God acting in history and exercising his righteous rule over all mankind. To call it a "kingdom" is to give the picture of a place, a country under God's rule. We would do better to think of the kingdom of God as "the rule of God"—of God reigning like a king over the whole creation.

We all belong to the kingdom of God and live under God's rule, although most people in this world refuse to acknowledge that this is so. The politician wrestling with the problems of his constituents, the businessman seeking to sell his products, the labor leader trying to represent the interests of the members of his union, the teacher attempting to mold the lives of pupils, the housewife, the machinist, the waitress, the porter, the salesman, the truck driver— each and every one lives under the rule of God. If our faith in God is to be without hypocrisy, then we must live our love for God as members of that kingdom to which all human society belongs; and if our daily actions are to be faithful to God, then we can never act without acknowledging the overarching rule of God. To believe in God is to produce acts of love toward our fellows. To live with our fellows in society is to test our faith in God.

The knowledge that this is the way the world is, that we belong to the kingdom of God, is what Jesus advised his disciples to seek above all things. Living in full consciousness of God's rule over life and in responsible relation to our neighbors is the treasure hidden in a field, the pearl of great value for which we should be willing to sell all that we have. Now we can see no more of this kingdom than a tiny mustard seed, but in time it will grow to fill the whole earth. All men belong to the kingdom of God, whether they know it or not, for it is like a net that gathers up fish of every kind. The knowledge of this kingdom is spread as far and wide as seed sown upon the ground, but only those soils which are prepared for it can bring forth fruit. This is the way Jesus described the kingdom of God to his disciples (see Matt., chap 13); and it is for this rule of God over all that Jesus asked them to pray:

"Thy kingdom come,
  Thy will be done,
    On earth as it is in heaven" (Matt. 6:10).

True faith and true living demand that we not only belong to the kingdom of God, but also know and acknowledge that we belong to it.

LIVING OUR FAITH

It is an easy matter for the preacher or the Bible scholar to talk this way, for his main concern is to show us what the Bible has to say about God and his rule over the world. But this lofty, over-all view does not say very much about how a person should act or what he should decide in specific situations. Most people want some guidance concerning what they should do, as well as what they should believe. The greatest problem is in *living* our faith.

The Bible is very disappointing to those who come to it asking, "What do you do in a case like this?" The Bible is not a rule book that gives neat answers for all the situations and problems that arise in life. The Bible is not a statement of lofty ideals which we are to strive for, but which we shall never reach. Instead, the Bible is a witness to the fact that God has acted and continues to act in the world; it is a summons to respond to what he is doing, to live consciously as citizens of the kingdom of God.

Yet in much of our life as Christians and in much of our organized action in society, we act as though we were under obligation to live by a set of rules or were committed to strive after impossible ideals. Much of our social action has been undertaken either from a sense of duty or a sense of aspiration, rather than from a faith in God who has made us and redeemed us. Many times we have done what needed to be done, but we have not done it for the deepest reasons or in the most faithful way. The way of duty and the way of aspiration have their merits, but there is a "more excellent way," the way of love and responsibility.

THE WAY OF DUTY

It is indeed possible so to read the Bible as to find in it a set of rules. The Ten Commandments, the Sermon on the

Mount and the other teachings of Jesus, and the exhortations of Paul can all be taken as rules to guide our living and our action in society. The difficulty is that the rules quickly come to take the place of the God who rules over all. The way of duty, when followed too closely, becomes the way of legalism.

We have seen already that the Ten Commandments and the other laws in the Old Testament were laws of the Covenant to help Israel live faithfully under God. Yet Jesus could save his harshest words for the scribes and Pharisees, those who were trying hardest to obey all the laws. This was because they had come to place obedience to a law above service to God or neighbor. For them it had become more important to keep the Sabbath than to minister to a human need on the Sabbath. They were more concerned to be obedient in every small particular of the Temple ritual than to take up the cause of the people of the land who languished in starvation and poverty. They were more interested in keeping themselves clean and holy through their religious observances than with examining the true state of their souls. (See particularly the "woes" which Jesus pronounced upon the scribes and Pharisees, Matt., chap 23.) The rules had become their god; the way of duty had become legalism.

The history of our own nation has many examples of good causes that became marred by the spirit of legalism in which they were undertaken. The abolition of slavery was a cause that needed to be undertaken. Even before the nation gained its independence, John Woolman of New Jersey had seen the need for all to live in America as free men. Attempts to extend slavery into the free territories of the West met increasing opposition from groups in the North who called themselves Abolitionists, and the Underground Railway was formed to help runaway slaves escape from their Southern masters. When the Civil War came, the Abolitionists welcomed it as a chance to do their duty, to set all the slaves free, and to punish the slaveholders. How different was the spirit of President Lincoln! Even at the height of the war, he was able to pray, asking whether God could be on either side when the cost was so much bloodshed. As the war came to a close, the legalists, who could only think of their duty to free the slaves, were planning the Reconstruction Acts to punish the South. President Lincoln, on the other hand, was telling the nation it must proceed "With malice toward none, with charity for all, with firmness in the right, as God gives us to see the right."

Life does, indeed, involve duty to "the right, as God gives us to see the right," but we must always be aware that we do not see all the right. Therefore, our knowledge of our duty is always partial. Any rules or laws we form for ourselves or our society on the basis of what we know are partial, too. We must be loyal and obedient to what we know, but we cannot follow the way of duty alone. That way lies legalism.

THE WAY OF ASPIRATION

Many people read the Bible and attend church in order to discover ideals and goals for life. Here again, it is easily possible to read the Bible and discover in it ideals and values after which man and his society should aspire. The difficulty is that we tend to postpone the achievement of these ideals to some future time, or to regard them as "impossible" of attainment. The way of aspiration, when followed too closely, becomes the way of idealism, visionary or disillusioned.

In Jesus' statements to his disciples and to the crowds that followed after him, a characteristic note is his emphasis on the present rather than the future. When a disciple wished to delay before following him, Jesus said, "Follow me, and leave the dead to bury their own dead" (Matt. 8:22). He spoke often of the Last Judgment and of the life in the age to come, but in the great parable of the Last Judgment (Matt. 25:31-46) it is those who feed the hungry, give drink to the thirsty, welcome the stranger, clothe the naked, visit the sick and the prisoner, who inherit "the kingdom prepared for you from the foundation of the world." This is the whole point of Jesus' statement to the Pharisees, "Behold, the kingdom of God is in the midst of you." The kingdom is now, the kingdom is here; the kingdom is not an ideal to be realized in some distant future.

The history of international communism is the story of idealism betrayed by itself. When Karl Marx wrote *Das Kapital,* he dealt with real problems in the industrial world of his day. Workers were not receiving their fair share of the fruits of their labor. Marx and his followers had a noble vision of a classless society in which all men would live equally. When men who believed in this principle took power in Russia in 1919, many idealists in other countries felt that the world was close to realizing a classless society. But the ideal remained an ideal—far in the distant future— as first Lenin, then Stalin, instituted bloody methods to hold the people in check. George Orwell in his fable, *Animal Farm,* has described the process by saying that the slogan, "All animals are equal," was changed to read, "All animals are equal, but some are *more equal* than others." As described by the ex-Communist theorist, Djilas of Yugoslavia, communism's pursuit of the classless society has produced a "new class" of party leaders who live off the rest of society with no check on what they do. Communism, for the idealists who had sought equality through it, has proved to be "the god that failed."

Life involves aspiration, dissatisfaction with that which is and the pursuit of that which could be. But we must be aware that God is more concerned with what we are doing at present than with where we say we are headed. Our aspiration is always in danger of being blind or misguided. The world is full of idealists who say their flags are still flying, but who, having given up all hope of reaching their goal, are merely marking time. We must seek a better life and a better society than that which we now have, but we cannot follow the way of aspiration alone. That way lies idealism, visionary or disillusioned.

THE WAY OF LOVE AND RESPONSIBILITY

The Bible is neither a rule book nor a statement of ideals. It is a witness to the fact that God has acted and continues to act in the world; it is a summons to us to respond to what he is doing in the present. The Bible calls us to follow a way that is more natural, and yet more strenuous, than the way of duty or the way of aspiration; namely, the way of love and responsibility.

When we approach a problem or tension in our common life, we must see it for what it really is. The way of duty tends to focus attention on what men have done in the past and to lay on us the obligation to do the same now. The way of aspiration tends to place our attention on the future and to tie all present action to what we hope it will produce. But the way of love and responsibility gives primary place to the present moment, the kingdom of God in our very midst.

Our lives are lived in relation both to God and to men. We are unfaithful to God if we do not acknowledge our responsibility to the society of which we are a part or do not know it as it is. The good Christian who walks the streets of his town by day and goes back into his own home at sunset without awareness of what happens on those same streets at night shares responsibility with the vice lords, the teen-age gang leaders, and the corrupt policemen and public officials for the crimes committed. The Christian who belongs to a union and pays his dues but never attends a meeting is responsible along with his union officers for the shortcomings and failures of the labor movement. The Christian woman who busies herself with good works and welfare activities through the local women's club or fraternal organization while remaining strictly "non-partisan" is doing her share to make it possible for small political cliques to dominate the life of her town. We need to know the life around us as it is.

In Christian social action a great deal of our time needs to be spent in finding out exactly what the world of men is like. We cannot begin to understand what are the problems we face—let alone what should be done about them—until we know the depth of our own involvement in the society in which we live. Every effort we make to learn more about politics, economics, social relations, welfare problems, and international affairs helps us to answer the question, "Who is my neighbor?" Also, it gives us greater ability to deal with the world as it is, rather than as it used to be or as we wish it would be. We are right when we sing, "This is my Father's world"; but it is a real world inhabited by real people, and we do not know our Father's world unless we know it that way.

This way of love and responsibility is not the shallow "realism" of those who say, "I deal with things as they really are," and then fail to take God into account. Right in the middle of the life we live, God is present and working. "Truly, I say to you, as you did it to one of the least of these my brethren, you did it to me" (Matt. 25:40). The people around us, with whom we work and for whom we try to secure a better life, are all "the brother for whom Christ died (1 Cor. 8:11). We need always to ask ourselves for what purpose God is working in any situation.

THE GRACE OF GOD AT WORK

The way of duty and the way of aspiration are both acutely conscious of how much God expects of us. Jesus makes this clear in the Sermon on the Mount when he compares the commandments of the Old Covenant with what is expected in the new life of freedom and grace (Matt. 5:21-47). What Jesus says, in effect, is this: "Being angry is the same as murder, lusting after a woman is the same as adultery, not swearing at all is better than false oaths, turning the other cheek is better than paying back a blow with a blow, and loving an enemy is better than hating him."

> "For I tell you, unless your righteousness exceeds that of the scribes and Pharisees, you will never enter the kingdom of heaven. . . . You, therefore, must be perfect, as your heavenly Father is perfect" (Matt. 5:20, 48).

Whether seen as a never-ending obligation (duty) or as a constant goal (aspiration), this call to perfection is a ceaseless judgment on our efforts to do good deeds. When we know that the Lord judges his people for all that they do, we can agree with the author of the Letter to the Hebrews: "It is a fearful thing to fall into the hands of the living God" (Heb. 10:31).

Knowing that God expects perfection, we know also that we are not perfect and do not perform perfect deeds. The fact of sin in our lives is as real after we know God's redemption in Christ as it was before. Paul, writing to the Romans, could speak thus about himself even after his conversion:

> "I do not understand my own actions. For I do not do what I want, but I do the very thing I hate. . . . For I do not do the

good I want, but the evil I do not want is what I do. Now if I do what I do not want, it is no longer I that do it, but sin which dwells within me. So I find it to be a law that when I want to do right, evil lies close at hand. For I delight in the law of God, in my inmost self, but I see in my members another law at work with the law of my mind and making me captive to the law of sin which dwells in my members. Wretched man that I am! Who will deliver me from this body of death?" (Rom. 7:15, 19-24).

Believing in the Lord Jesus Christ does not make us perfect; rather, God's grace through faith in Jesus Christ makes it possible for us to live with imperfection when we know that the ultimate issue is in God's hands. Trusting in God's grace, we are willing to respond to what we know of his will and to keep on seeking to know it more perfectly.

"There is therefore now no condemnation for those who are in Christ Jesus. For the law of the Spirit of life in Christ Jesus has set me free from the law of sin and death" (Rom. 8:1-2).

By the death of his Son upon the cross, God already has taken upon himself the consequences of our sin and has freed us to live a life that responds to his will.

This strikes to the heart of one of the most crucial problems in Christian social action. Time and again study groups and action groups fail to follow through on issues that they can clearly see demand action. Unable to do "the right thing," they end up doing nothing. In fact, what they have been doing is waiting for the perfect time to do the perfect thing. Faith in the Lord Jesus Christ does more than affect our personal lives; it also frees us as groups of Christians to go ahead and do the best we know, trusting that God's grace can forgive the efforts which are imperfect or misdirected.

In plain truth, most of the issues which face us in our

personal lives and also in our lives in society are not black-and-white issues in which good and the will of God stand directly opposed by evil and the designs of Satan. They are all varying shades of gray, and they ask us to make partial decisions and relative judgments about them. One great temptation is to take one side of an important issue and place on it the label, "Christian," forgetting that it may be only partially right and that there may be truth and worth on the other side too.

We must decide, for to believe in a God who acts and who asks for righteousness is to believe that we must be doers as well as hearers of the word. Knowing the actual situation as fully as we can and responding as fully as we can to what we know of God's will, we must act. But whether the issue be one of world peace, of the use of alcohol, of the choice of political party affiliation, or of racial understanding, we can be sure that we will do God's will imperfectly and may even choose the wrong side. Therefore, our prayer always should be thus:

> "O God, who rulest all our days and hast given us thy Son to redeem our lives from destruction: help us to know that on all sides great issues call upon us for decision and action; grant that we may with sober mind and firm purpose respond to the calling of thy will; and when we have done what we could, forgive us by thy grace for all that we have done amiss or failed to do; we ask in the name of Jesus Christ, who in every respect has been tempted as we are, yet without sinning. Amen."

For Your Personal Meditation and Study

James 1:22-25; 2:14-26. Martin Luther emphasized that it was "by faith alone" that a man is saved. Of what importance, then, are the works that we do?

Luke 17:20-21. Some translations of the New Testament have here, "The kingdom of God is within you";

others have, "The kingdom of God is in the midst of you." Does it make a real difference which way the words are translated? Which way do you feel is correct?

Matthew 13:1-50. Matthew regularly uses the phrase "kingdom of heaven" rather than "kingdom of God." Why do you think he does so? What do these parables tell you about the kind of kingdom this is?

Matthew 6:7-15. What does it mean to you when you pray in the Lord's Prayer, "Thy kingdom come"? Does this show that the kingdom is not in the present?

Matthew 5:1-48. Read this whole chapter through at one time. Do you feel that Jesus was giving us a new Law to take the place of the one given "to the men of old"? Do you feel that what he is giving is an ideal toward which we must strive? Is it possible or impossible to fulfill what Jesus asks here?

Romans 7:15; 8:2. Has your experience of the Christian life coincided with Paul's, or do you find it possible to do the good you want to do? In what way does being "in Christ Jesus" make it easier to do good?

For Thought and Discussion

1. Can you think of social problems with respect to which your church and its members have been inactive? What were the reasons for this inactivity?

2. What does your church do to help its members be "doers" as well as "hearers"?

3. Where do you look for the kingdom of God and knowledge of God's will for human life, within your own heart or in what is happening in the world around you?

4. Give examples of evidence that God's kingdom is in the life of the world we live in.

5. Many Christians go to the Bible for guidance in matters of faith and conduct. Can we expect the Bible to tell us what to do when dealing with particular social issues? What kind of help should we expect from the Bible?

6. Give examples of legalism that has occurred when church people have dealt with social issues. Give examples of idealism. Do you feel that the latter was the best way to deal with those problems?

7. In what way are we as Christians expected to follow the way of duty? The way of aspiration?

8. Is a man expected to be righteous only in his personal life, or do the teachings of Jesus about righteousness extend to his social life also?

9. Why is it especially necessary for Christians to understand the technical aspects of social problems in which they are involved and with respect to which they would act?

10. Augustine said, "Love God, and do as you please." What did he mean? Does trusting in God's grace mean not caring about what you do, so long as you do something?

5

THE CHURCH AND THE WORLD

As CHRISTIANS we are members of the Church, the Body of Christ. As Christians we are members also of a particular local church. When we call ourselves "members" of the Church, we do not mean merely that we have joined it and become members of it, as one might join a club; we mean that we all are joined together in fellowship like the members of a body. "Now you are the body of Christ and individually members of it" (1 Cor. 12:27).

But we are members also of the society in which we live. We reside in a particular town and state. We belong to a particular economic and social group. We all are Americans by nationality. We all share the heritage of Western civilization. Therefore, we cannot live our lives as if our only membership were in the Church. We are members also of the world, and the way in which we view the relationship of our membership in the world to our membership in Christ can make a great deal of difference for the way in which we undertake Christian social action.

"WORLD" IN THE BIBLE

The Bible is never so taken up with the work of God through the chosen people Israel, through the Savior Jesus Christ, and through the fellowship of the Church that it fails to take account of the existence of human society outside of Israel and the Church. The books of the Old Testa-

75

ment make constant reference to "the nations" and "the peoples" outside of Israel. The customary Hebrew word for these other people is *goyim,* which the King James Version translates as "heathen." The Psalms are full of references to these non-Israelites. Two brief passages will serve to illustrate this use of the word:

> "Why do the nations [*goyim*] conspire,
>   and the peoples plot in vain?" (Ps. 2:1).

> "May God be gracious to us and bless us
>   and make his face to shine upon us,
> that thy way may be known upon earth,
>   thy saving power among all nations [*goyim*].
> Let the peoples praise thee, O God;
>   let all the peoples praise thee!" (Ps. 67:1-3).

All the rest of the world, the world outside of and surrounding Israel, is spoken of as "nations," "peoples," "kings."

These nations also have been created by God. The story of the covenant with Noah (Gen., chaps. 9-10) shows us Israel's conviction that all races and nations had a common ancestry, and the story of Babel (Gen., chap. 11) makes it plain that their language has been confused and that they have been scattered abroad over the face of all the earth. In a way, the King James Version's translation of *goyim* as "heathen" is appropriate, for these people have denied God and gone after idols. But we must be careful to understand that the Jews thought of these "nations" and "peoples" as being the countries which surrounded them.

> "Declare his glory among the nations [*goyim*],
>   his marvelous works among all the peoples!
> For great is the Lord, and greatly to be praised;
>   he is to be feared above all gods.
> For all the gods of the peoples are idols;
>   but the Lord made the heavens" (Ps. 96:3-5)

The same God ruled over Jew and Gentile alike; but only Israel knew who he was.

We have already seen (chap. 3) that the New Testament looks at the world differently. The word *kosmos,* adopted from the vocabulary of everyday Greek, means the universe, the whole inhabited earth, the world of men. The "nations" and "peoples" of the Old Testament are replaced by "the world," a more general word, speaking of all of human society.

The world, like the nations and peoples, is God's creation. John can speak of Jesus Christ in this way:

> "The true light that enlightens every man was coming into the world; he was in the world [*kosmos*], and the world was made through him, yet the world knew him not" (John 1:9-10).

But the world, again like the nations and peoples, also is alienated from God. The various letters in the New Testament refer often to "principalities," "powers," "rulers of this age." The world is believed to be in the hands of Satan and his demons. So, the tempter could offer Jesus "the kingdoms of the world" when he showed them to him from a high mountain (Matt. 4:8-10). In the world, men do not honor God or give thanks to him, but worship idols instead, the creature rather than the Creator. Paul, in the Letter to the Romans, gives a searching description of the baseness of this life in its opposition to God (Rom. 1:18-32). Yet it is this same world into which Christ came and for which he died.

THE CHURCH AGAINST THE WORLD

Anyone seeking to understand the relation between the Church and the world must first recognize that the early Church, as shown in the pages of the New Testament, believed that the two were in eternal opposition to each other. They could envision no possible relation other than *the Church against the world*. The letters of John state this position as strongly as any passages in the Bible.

> "Do not love the world or the things in the world. If any one loves the world, love for the Father is not in him. For all that is in the world, the lust of the flesh and the lust of the eyes and the pride of life, is not of the Father but is of the world. And the world passes away, and the lust of it; but he who does the will of God abides forever" (1 John 2:15-17).

The Church has no part with the world, and the world has no part with the Church. Where this point of view prevails, to be a member of the world is to be disqualified as a member of the Church, and vice versa.

It is easy to understand why the Church in apostolic times engaged in this policy of "isolationism." Its members lived in a hostile pagan society. Their only protection lay in being considered by the Roman government to be a Jewish sect, but they encountered even greater hostility from the Jews. (See, for example, the treatment Paul and Barnabas received at Iconium, as related in Acts 14:1-7.) Their numbers were small, their strength was weak. Therefore, these churches concentrated upon the cultivation of holiness within their fellowship and the gaining of new members, leaving the world to destruction.

When the Church sees itself in opposition to the world, there is no place for Christian social action. Quietism, the passive acceptance of things as they are, becomes the only way for Christians to deal with the world. Time and again in Christian history members of the Church have adopted this strategy. The early monks withdrew from the chaotic world left by the fall of Rome. The Anabaptists gathered their followers out of the world and lived a separated life. In our own day, many sects and small groups of Christian people, despairing of the world in which they live, refuse to have anything to do with the world. This leads them into strange incongruities. The Amish are divided between those who will use only hooks and eyes on their clothes, as did their forefathers in Germany, and those who will use the world's new invention of buttons. Some still drive buggies, while others are willing to drive simple, black automobiles. But Wesleyans, who refuse to wear short sleeves, jewelry, or make-up, are willing to buy the gaudiest of the new hard-tops, and Gospel sects which proclaim their freedom from the world will display in a prominent place on the wall of their assembly room a picture of the President of the United States.

The Church in our day is not the Church of the New Testament, for we do not live in New Testament times. In many countries Christians are no longer a minority, although in the world's population they are still a minority. The Church and its members must share responsibility for the whole development of Western civilization since the fall of Rome. In America we must share responsibility for the whole framework of government and society. In apostolic times, and even up until the rule of Constantine, the Church could maintain that it had no part in the culture around it. But the Church against the world is not a strategy for our time. There are other possibilities open to us; we can engage in responsible social action.

THE CHURCH OF THE WORLD

To deny that the Church must always be seen in opposition to the world is not to deny that there is tension between the two. But there have been times in Christian history when it has become difficult to distinguish between the Church and the world, when the Church, in fact, has become *the Church of the world.*

"In every culture to which the Gospel comes there are men who hail Jesus as the Messiah of their society, the fulfiller of its hopes and aspirations, the perfecter of its true faith, the source of its holiest spirit."[1]

In the new condition of history, not known by the Church of the New Testament, when the Church ceases to be a minority and must come to some reckoning with the world, men have allowed the Body of Christ to become a "worldly Church."

The worldly Church has taken many forms. It has been the folk-church, the tribal church, the racial church, or the national church. It has produced feudalist and capitalist and Marxist Christianity. It has been nationalist, and it has been internationalist. It has used its faith sometimes to justify the virtue of the privileged and sometimes the virtue of the disinherited. Whatever form it has taken, the worldly Church has turned the object of the Church's work from the worship and service of God to the exaltation and self-protection of men and their systems. Such a church will engage in social action, but it is only action designed to preserve and extend the status quo rather than to transform and improve it.

Here lies the greatest problem for our present-day American churches: we are in constant peril of becoming the Church of the world, the worldly Church. Our whole society places great value on conformity. The mind of the group takes precedence over the conscience and life of the individual. Our churches, accordingly, are under constant pressure to be just another organization among the many in town. They are expected to find their place along with the service clubs, fraternal groups, veterans' organizations, and women's clubs, and to take their share in the mainte-

[1] From *Christ and Culture*, by H. Richard Niebuhr. Page 83. Copyright, 1951, by Harper & Brothers. Used by permission.

nance of American society. Our national leaders make much use of Christian symbols and phrases. A political speech always seems to have to end with the mention of God. Yet our society is not becoming any more Christian. Rather, the churches seem to be conforming to the American culture around them and serving the masters of nation, worldly abundance, and group fulfillment.

The Bible warns against the worldly Church. "Do not be conformed to this world," Paul tells the Romans, "but be transformed by the renewal of your mind, that you may prove what is the will of God, what is good and acceptable and perfect" (Rom. 12:2). The Church has surrendered to the world when it allows itself to become the Church of the world. And every Church in every age is in danger of becoming conformist.

THAT THE WORLD MIGHT BE SAVED

Our present situation and the teaching of the Bible clearly rule out both an absolute opposition between the Church and the world (the Church against the world) and an absolute identity between the two (the Church of the world). The relation between the two is far more complex, and we shall have to find other and vastly better strategies for Christian social action than the simple ones of quietism or conformity.

Although the Church of the New Testament adopted the strategy of withdrawal from the world, the gospel proclaimed in the New Testament speaks of God's abiding love and concern for that same world.

"For God so *loved the world* that he gave his only Son, that whoever believes in him should not perish but have eternal life. For God sent the Son *into the world,* not to condemn the world, but *that the world might be saved* through him" (John 3:16-17).

There has been hostility between God and the world, hostility caused by the consequences of sin. But this hostility has never altered the fact that God made the world. His desire has been that the world might be saved, that it might be brought back to him. So, "God was in Christ reconciling the world to himself" (2 Cor. 5:19). God and the world, formerly torn asunder, have been brought back together in Jesus Christ. The rule of God over his world, the kingdom of God which had never ceased to exist, now is made plain for all to see. "The kingdom of the world has become the kingdom of our Lord and of his Christ" (Rev. 11:15). If God has such great concern for the world of men, then the Church should have it too.

In fact, in the eyes of God there are not two separate spheres of life here—Church and world; there is but one reality, the rule of God over the world now made plain in Jesus Christ. As members of the Church, we know that God has redeemed the world, and we know that all men stand in relation both to God and to other men. Others do not know this yet; but it is still a real fact in their lives, whether they wish to acknowledge God or not.

There are many pictures by which this relation between the Church and the world can be explained. Jesus himself spoke of the kingdom of God as like wheat and weeds (tares) growing up together, and not able to be separated until the harvest (Matt. 13:24-30). Some have spoken of life as having both a horizontal dimension (relation to men) and a vertical dimension (relation to God); the Church consists of those who know and consciously live in the vertical as well as the horizontal. Bishop Anders Nygren of Sweden has described the situation of men in the world as like that of men in hiding because they belonged to the underground resistance movement during the war. Some knew that their liberators had already landed and that the war would soon be over; others did not know that the decisive battles had been fought, and so they were still fighting desperately without hope. Christians know that their Liberator, Jesus Christ, has come, that the decisive battles against evil have been fought, and that the conclusion of the war will find their God victorious. God sent his Son "that the world might be saved," and the Church is composed of those who know that it has been saved.

THE WORLD IN THE CHURCH AND THE CHURCH IN THE WORLD

As members of the Church we are at the same time members of the world. This means there is always a great deal of *the world in the Church.* Although we are accustomed to speaking of the Church in its fullest dimensions as the Body of Christ, we must admit that it is impossible to defend everything we find in the life of the churches as coming from God; a great deal of it comes from the particular society in which these churches live. In our American churches, our concern for placing everything "on a sound financial basis," our exaltation of lay organizations in the church even over the worship of the congregation, our tendency to give the chief places in the life of the church to those who occupy the chief places in the life of our community, our emphasis on liberty without a corresponding interest in justice and equality—all these are as much marks of our being Americans as they are marks of our being Christians.

We cannot avoid having some of the world in the Church. The churches of a country in Southeast Asia or Africa necessarily will take a different form and hold different views than the churches of Europe or South America, and these will be different from the churches of the United States. The churches of previous periods of history, because they shared in the life of their world, differed from the churches of today; and we cannot expect that the churches a century from now will be the same as those today. Our problem is to keep the world from dominating the churches, to keep from having a worldly Church.

The record of the churches in time of war and international conflict shows how difficult it is to prevent the world from controlling the actions of the Church. In Nazi Germany there was the German Church, which fully supported Hitler, while only a small minority in the Confessing Church refused to back his regime and policies. At the same time in America we sang a song about the fighting chaplain at Pearl Harbor who manned a gun and said, "Praise the Lord, and pass the ammunition." At the present time, it is difficult to find churchmen, whether in Communist or non-Communist countries, who will criticize the basic approach of their nation to international affairs. It is very difficult to avoid having our national loyalty—or, for that matter, our economic, social, or racial loyalty—influence the decisions and actions we make as Christians. The world is in the Church.

At the same time, there is an unrecognized *Church in the world*. God's redeeming work is known and acknowledged most fully by those in the churches, but we make a mistake if we assume that this work is carried on solely through our churches and by their members. By their work the doctor, the scientist, the inventor, the artist, the humanitarian, the journalist, the politician, the businessman, and the union leader all have made contributions to the advancement of the cause of God's kingdom. A World Health Organization doctor injecting natives of a tropical country with penicillin to prevent yaws has his place in God's redeeming work in their lives, along with the evangelist who brings them the story of the Bible. The social worker, be he

Christian or not, who offers friendship and direction to the member of a teen-age gang or to an older person without family shares in the work of God. God, who could use Artaxerxes to restore his people to the Land of Promise, can surely use the life and work of the whole world to accomplish his redemptive purpose.

The meaning of all this for Christian social action is very simple and very clear. Because the world is in the Church, we must always be careful to examine ourselves to discover whether the action we are considering is of men or of God, whether it is a cloak for self-interest or a real benefit to those for whom it is done. We must be willing to recognize that whatever we do will be influenced by who we are in the world and what we believe as members of the world. The Church is also in the world. This means that we should never assume that it is up to Christian people and the Christian churches to perform every act of service for the world. It also means that we should not deprecate the work of others who are not Christians, for what they are doing may have greater place in the redeeming work of God than our halfhearted efforts. Let us not exalt what we do because it is "Christian"; let us acknowledge that more belongs to Christ than we can even imagine.

THE SERVANT OF THE WORLD

The role of the Church in the world is to witness to the world about its true state. If God loved this world and has given his Son to save it, then we too should love it. The Church and its members are called to be the servant of the world. This is made clear in Jesus' words to his disciples:

> "'If any one would be first, he must be last of all and servant of all.' And he took a child, and put him in the midst of them; and taking him in his arms, he said to them, 'Whoever receives one such child in my name receives me'" (Mark 9:35-37).

Paul has written of how Jesus' own life added weight to these words.

> "Do nothing from selfishness or conceit, but in humility count others better than yourselves. Let each of you look not only to his own interests, but also to the interests of others. Have this mind among yourselves, which you have in Christ Jesus, who, though he was in the form of God, did not count equality with God a thing to be grasped, but emptied himself, taking the form of a servant, being born in the likeness of men. And being found in human form he humbled himself and became obedient unto death, even death on a cross" (Phil. 2:3-8).

Christ "emptied himself" and took the form of a servant, he "humbled himself" and became obedient unto death, for the sake of the world. The Church cannot expect to do differently than its Master and Lord.

The exact character of this relation between the Church and the world is difficult to describe. H. Richard Niebuhr, in his book *Christ and Culture*,[1] has traced three different approaches to the problem which have been adopted by different Churches at different times. His analysis may be summed up as follows:

1. *Christ above culture* (the Church above the world). This is the position of the Roman Catholic Church, found most clearly stated in the writings of Thomas Aquinas. All through the life of the world there is evidence of God's work, but the final redemption comes from the Church, which stands above the world.

2. *Christ and culture in paradox* (the Church and the world in tension). This was the position taken by Martin Luther, who stated there are separate areas of Law and Gospel in human life, and that these do not overlap, but complement each other. Such a view takes seriously the

[1] Adapted from *Christ and Culture*, by H. Richard Niebuhr. Copyright, 1951, by Harper & Brothers. Used by permission.

existence of sin in the world, but it tends to overlook sin in the church.

3. *Christ transforming culture* (the Church redeeming the world). Here the work of the Church is thought to be in the middle of the world, where God's redeeming work is being carried on.

All three approaches are agreed that the members of the Church must undertake responsibility for the society in which they live and must work for its improvement. Social action is a part of the calling of a Christian man and of the church to which he belongs.

THE MEANS BY WHICH WE ACT

It is often argued that we as Christians must be sure to use Christian means when we act in society. By this it usually is meant that the spirit in which action is taken should be peaceable, open-minded, humble, and the like. However, the truth of the matter is that, although we should always seek to act in a spirit of Christian love and brotherhood, the means we use are always *the world's means;* there are no special avenues of action available to Christians and to nobody else. The problems of the world must be dealt with and solved in the arena of the world; this means using the world's means. This is one way in which we can understand Jesus' teaching about paying taxes to Caesar: "Render therefore to Caesar the things that are Caesar's, and to God the things that are God's" (Matt. 22:21). As Caesar's coin must be used to pay Caesar's tax, so the world's methods must be used when we undertake to deal with the world's problems.

When Christians are involved in the complexities of an economic problem, they do not bring to that problem any special competence because they are Christians. It is necessary to use the theories of economics to understand the problem, and to use the institutions of the economic life to deal with it. In every area of human life the Christian, like everyone else, must employ all the resources of human intellect and understanding to search out the causes and ramifications of a problem; and the Christian, like everyone else, must work through the means that lie at hand in everyday life. Politics, economics, social welfare, international affairs —whatever the sphere of life—the means by which we act are the world's means. We are mistaken if we assume that these means are evil or less good because they are not the special property of Christians.

In Christian social action we can act either through our churches in groups organized for social action or through the life of everyday in the various roles we play in society— employer, employee, parent, citizen, neighbor, world citizen. But we are mistaken if we feel that there is something *more* "Christian" about the action we take through our church, for the world is in the church and the church acts as a part of the world. All that we do in our various other roles in society counts as much as what is done specifically in the name of the church; and this kind of natural action, whether by individuals or groups, can be as great an expression of God's will for his world as what the churches do in their special activities.

The difference in Christian social action is not in the means by which we act; they are the world's means. The difference is in the perspective in which the Christian sees his action. The Christian knows that the world is redeemed and that he labors in the sight of God as well as of men. This gives him a hope that others do not possess.

> "Then the seventh angel blew his trumpet, and there were loud voices in heaven, saying, 'The kingdom of the world has become the kingdom of our Lord and of his Christ, and he shall reign for ever and ever.' And the twenty-four elders who

sit on their thrones before God fell on their faces and worshiped God, saying,
'We give thanks to thee, Lord God almighty, who art and who
     wast,
     that thou hast taken thy great power and begun to reign.
The nations raged, but thy wrath came,
     and the time for the dead to be judged,
for rewarding thy servants, the prophets and saints,
     and those who fear thy name, both small and great,
and for destroying the destroyers of earth'" (Rev. 11:15-18).

This is the hope which sustained the Church of an earlier
day in the time of persecution, and it is the hope which can
sustain the Church of our day in its action in the world.

For Your Personal Meditation and Study

Psalm 96. This Psalm was sung by the people of Israel.
Notice how they were confident that God had made the
heavens and the earth. Does the Lord reign over Israel only
or over the "peoples" and "nations" also?

1 John 2:1-6, 15-17. Jesus Christ is the expiation "for
the sins of the whole world," not only for those in the
Church. Why does the writer go on to advise his readers not
to love "the world"?

Romans 12:1-8. The life of a Christian in the Church
is the life of a member in the Body of Christ. What does
Paul mean by being "conformed to this world"? By being
"transformed by the renewal of your mind"?

John 3:16-21. John says that the light "has come into
the world" in Jesus Christ. Can the world ever be the same
after God's Son has come into it? God loved "the world";
are we asked to do the same?

Philippians 2:1-11. "No cross, no crown," runs the old
saying. Would the world have been saved if Jesus had not
come as its servant and been obedient unto death? Is Paul

urging the Philippians to be servants of the world or of each other?

Matthew 22:15-22. Some have used this passage to justify "the Church against the world" position. How do you understand what Jesus says about "the things that are Caesar's" and "the things that are God's"? Is there anything in life which does not belong to God?

For Thought and Discussion

1. The Old Testament speaks of the "nations" or "heathen." Can we divide up the present world into heathen nations and Christian nations?

2. The New Testament speaks of the "world." Is this a different perspective than the Old Testament's "nations," "peoples," and "kingdoms"?

3. Give examples of present-day Christian groups that take the "Church against the world" position. Can they truly escape the influence of the society to which they belong?

4. Give examples of groups that have become "the Church of the world." In what ways have they allowed the gospel they preached to become conformed to the society to which they belong?

5. Can a church group in twentieth-century America be justified in maintaining the "Church against the world" or the "Church of the world" position?

6. Do you agree that the Church and the world overlap? In what ways?

7. Is the Church justified in distinguishing itself from the rest of human society?

8. The world is in the Church and the Church is in the world. Can you give examples of each situation?

9. Some would say that the Church has been set over the world to rule it. Do you believe the church is the master of the world or the servant of the world?

10. Are there any special "Christian" methods in social action? If not, what does it mean to speak of "Christian social action"?

11. Give examples of social action by church groups; by church members in their vocations in society. As Christians, are we expected to use both methods of action? Is there one which is more effective than the other?

6

HISTORY AND THE END OF HISTORY

EVERY LIVING THING has its atmosphere. We know that men and animals depend on the oxygen in the air, while plants require carbon dioxide. On other planets, whatever life there is, breathes an atmosphere different from that on earth. This atmosphere is taken for granted, yet the kind of atmosphere which a living thing needs determines the kind of life it leads. As human beings we all must live in an atmosphere containing oxygen, but we also live in an atmosphere of time—completely invisible though measured by clocks, taken for granted yet absolutely indispensable for human life.

The way in which we live our lives depends on the way we think of time. Most of our modern attitudes about time —the ideas prevailing in our Western world—came from the ancient Greeks. They held that only history and human life are in the realm of time; all else—God, nature, eternity—is in a realm of timelessness. Human history goes round and round in its old ways, surrounded on all sides by the Abyss of Eternity, which was before history and will be after history. The real meaning of life, according to this view, cannot be found in history; it lies with the timeless God who dwells in a timeless eternity. It does not take much imagination to see that this is very much like what some Christians mean when they talk about heaven as their home. Life in time has ceased to have much meaning to them.

But the Bible speaks of life in time as being supremely important. The biblical faith is completely "historical" and always speaks of God and eternity in terms of time. There are two important characteristics of time, according to the Bible: 1. Time moves in one direction only—that is, forward; and it cannot be reversed or abolished. 2. Time has been changed by the coming of Jesus Christ. According to the Bible, God and eternity are as much in the atmosphere of time as we are. Therefore, the way we look at time can make a great difference in the way in which we live in it.

LIFE BETWEEN THE AGES

God does not dwell in some timelessness outside of history and time. The Bible looks back to a beginning and forward to an end. Whether we read the Book of Genesis or the Gospel of John, we see that there has been time for as far back as we can see, all the way to "the beginning."

"In the beginning God created the heavens and the earth" (Gen. 1:1).
"In the beginning was the Word, and the Word was with God, and the Word was God. He was in the beginning with God . . ." (John 1:1-2).

History goes back in a series of ages to a beginning, and the Bible can conceive of nothing as existing before that time.

But history also looks forward to an end. When the Bible speaks of "for ever and ever" or "world without end," it does not mean a timeless extension at the end of history. The Greek words could be literally translated "to the age" or "to the age of the ages." In front of us in history there is more time, ages and ages of it, that will last until there is a final end.

Our life, then, is a life between the ages. History has already had its beginning. Ages have passed since that time.

We cannot return to that beginning, for all time now continues to move toward its end, an end that will be reached in time, not in some timeless eternity. This means that for us as Christians history and the life we are living at the present moment are of supreme importance; they are important because they are part of the sphere of God's activity. Our life is not a meaningless episode to be passed over when we are set free by death for a timeless eternity. Our present labors, like the labors of all those who have gone before us, have their part in the course of life as it moves forward through time. We should not feel insignificant when we look back through the ages to the beginning and forward to the end. Our life between the ages is of supreme importance to God, who is ever mindful of us and who lives "to the age of the ages."

"WHEN THE TIME HAD FULLY COME"

We live not only "between the ages" but also "in the year of the Lord." The early Church, fairly soon in its history, recognized that the coming of Jesus Christ had changed the course of the world. The term *Anno Domini* (Latin for "year of the Lord") began to be used, and all dates were figured from the estimated date of Christ's birth. In this the Church has been no different from other groups in human history that have felt that history has made a new beginning. The Romans figured dates "from the beginning of the City" (A.U.C., *ab urbe condita*). The French Revolution dated its new calendar from the day of the proclamation of the First Republic, while the Soviet Union measures time from the October Revolution of 1917. However, it is surprising to discover that it was not until recent centuries that men began also to figure time back from the birth of Christ and to speak of B.C. (Before Christ) as well as A.D. (Anno Domini). It took men longer to realize that Christ was not only the beginning of a new era but also the high point and climax of all history.

Paul, who as a Jew had formerly looked forward to a climax of history that he hoped was coming, realized after his conversion that the time had fully come (King James Version: "in the fulness of time") when Jesus was born.

> "When we were children, we were slaves to the elemental spirits of the universe. But when the time had fully come, God sent forth his Son, born of woman, born under the law, to redeem those who were under the law, so that we might receive adoption as sons" (Gal. 4:3-5).

Christ came to fulfill and complete the revelation of God's redeeming work in history. Before Christ came, the world was incomplete; now that he has come, it can never be the same again.

History, for the Christian, has not only a beginning and an end; it has also a climax which has already occurred. We who live in "the year of the Lord" are citizens of a new age. History has already reached its fullness in Jesus Christ. This sense of living in the new age is very strong in the letters of the New Testament. Here is an example from the letter to the Hebrews:

> "Therefore, brethren, since we have confidence to enter the sanctuary by the blood of Jesus, by the new and living way which he opened for us through the curtain, that is, through his flesh, and since we have a great priest over the house of God, let us draw near with a true heart in full assurance of faith. . . . Let us hold fast the confession of our hope without wavering, for he who promised is faithful; and let us consider how to stir up one another to love and good works, not neglecting to meet together, as is the habit of some, but encouraging one another, and all the more as you see the Day drawing near" (Heb. 10:19-25).

Christ has opened a "new and living way" between man and God; the two can no longer be considered estranged from each other. Men can draw near to God "in full assurance of faith." Now they work and wait for "the Day of the Lord" when the end will come.

Such a view of history not only rules out the ancient Greek view that the history of the world is a succession of cycles in which the same patterns repeat themselves over and over again. It also raises questions about the progress theory that sees all history as moving "onward and upward" to better things, and the golden age theory that sees all history as a corruption of some primitive pattern of perfection. History, for the Christian, is divided into two ages: the old age before Christ and the new age now that he has come. Henceforward, we cannot work as if he had not come.

THE HOPE TO WHICH GOD HAS CALLED US

In our social action we shall be working together with many different people and groups, not all of whom view history as we do. Some work with the feeling that what they are doing is meaningless, because it has been done many times before and will need to be done again after they are gone. Trapped by the fatalism of a cyclical view of time, they do their work without hope. Others, knowing that the work they do can never be completed in their lifetime, lose heart and yearn to see the end of their labors. Creatures of time, they yearn for timelessness.

Still others work with hope, but it is the false hope of progress. Believing that time not only moves in one direction but that it also moves steadily upward, they look forward to the world's getting better and better. This kind of hope has been strong in the various social movements in America. Groups have felt that if only slavery were abolished, if only economic exploitation were eliminated, or if only racial justice were established, we would have a better world. But their hopes have been dashed as successive generations have discovered that the elimination of one problem brings other problems in its wake. And the progress which they hoped would be steady and upward seems to be irregular and sporadic.

The hope with which the Christian labors is real, but it is not the false hope of progress. It is hope grounded in faith in the Lord Jesus Christ, who already has come and redeemed us. It is hope that recognizes that history will not be complete until the end of the age, and that we shall not have full fellowship with God until history is completed. Paul's letter to the Corinthians puts it in these memorable words:

> "For our knowledge is imperfect and our prophecy is imperfect; but when the perfect comes, the imperfect will pass away. . . . For now we see in a mirror dimly, but then face to face. Now I know in part; then I shall understand fully, even as I have been fully understood" (1 Cor. 13:9-10, 12).

We should not expect to see the completion of our labors, the fulfillment of all for which we work; this is not hope, says Paul in another place:

> "We know that the whole creation has been groaning in travail together until now; and not only the creation, but we ourselves, who have the first fruits of the Spirit, groan inwardly as we wait for adoption as sons, the redemption of our bodies. For in this hope we were saved. Now hope that is seen is not hope. For who hopes for what he sees? But if we hope for what we do not see, we wait for it with patience" (Rom. 8:22-25).

As Christians we may work together with others who do not share this hope, but we can never abandon this hope grounded in Christ and God for the shallow hopes of progress.

How relevant this Christian hope is to the work of Christian social action is made plain in this thoughtful statement by Donald B. Cloward, the first secretary of the Council on Christian Social Progress of the American Baptist Convention:

> "The call to Christian action is not a call to bring in the kingdom on one's own shoulders. Indeed the kingdom of God is not dependent upon us. God moves in a mysterious way. We are not even called upon to win great victories in the cause of Christ. But we are called upon to witness to the reality of that kingdom. Moreover we must learn to accept the fact that so much of our striving is doomed to defeat; causes we support never quite come off. Our own ego often blinds us to the true meaning of Christian faith and action. Mixed motives, a sense of self importance, an unawareness of our own sins have often tempted us to play God. Sober second thoughts therefore may serve to remind us that the ends are in God's hands, and it may be our highest service to Him lies just here. Not that we have attained anything significant or made any really worthwhile contribution to the cause of Christ. This is not required of us. But one thing is required of each of us as followers of the Christ—that we make the effort; are found where the battle is being waged and then having done all, to stand. For this may be our highest gain. The ends are with God."[1]

This is the hope with which a Christian labors; this is the hope to which we have been called. Those who cherish it will not be disappointed.

A NEW HEAVEN AND A NEW EARTH

So much has been said about the Christian's personal hope of immortality that many have forgotten that this hope is often presented in the Bible in social as well as in individualistic terms. The Jews looked forward to a restored Israel and a time when God would reside in his holy hill, Mount Zion. Jeremiah spoke of a New Covenant between God and his people (Jer. 31:31-34). Ezekiel saw a vision

[1] Donald B. Cloward, in *News Briefs for Action.* July-August, 1956.

of a restored Temple in the midst of a holy land (Ezek. 40:48). Isaiah saw the hope to be a perfect community in the city of Jerusalem.

> "For behold, I create new heavens
>   and a new earth;
> and the former things shall not be remembered
>   or come into mind.
> But be glad and rejoice for ever
>   in that which I create;
> for behold, I create Jerusalem a rejoicing,
>   and her people a joy.
> I will rejoice in Jerusalem,
>   and be glad in my people;
> no more shall be heard in it the sound of weeping
>   and the cry of distress" (Isa. 65:17-19).

This description of the new Jerusalem is idyllic: everyone will live out his days; everyone will live in the house he builds himself and eat the food he grows; neither they nor their children shall know fruitless work or calamity; and God will hear their every word and answer them. Not only do we live in close relation to our neighbor in this life; we must expect the relation to continue in the life of the age to come.

The New Testament does not do much to alter this communal nature of hope. The Revelation to John also looks forward to a restored heaven and earth and the life of a city.

> "Then I saw a new heaven and a new earth; for the first heaven and the first earth had passed away, and the sea was no more. And I saw the holy city, new Jerusalem, coming down out of heaven from God, prepared as a bride adorned for her husband; and I heard a great voice from the throne saying, 'Behold, the dwelling of God is with men. He will dwell with them, and they shall be his people, and God himself shall be with them . . .'" (Rev. 21:1-3).

Note that "the former things have passed away," and that all the society of men has been restored to its proper relation at the feet of God.

Hope like this makes social action worth while. It is hard to understand why the Christian church and its members should be spending all their days worrying about their individual lives and forgetting the life of society, when the life of the world to come will also be a society. We labor in society in the hope that the kingdom of God which we can dimly perceive in the midst of us will come in its glory and we shall all be able to live more fully the life which now we live so incompletely.

THE SHEEP AND THE GOATS

Having come this far, we now are ready to look at three passages with which we are all very familiar, but which have new meaning when we read them in the light of the Bible's point of view. The first is the parable of the Last Judgment (Matt. 25:31-46). This parable shows clearly what we have been saying about history and the end of history.

> "When the Son of man comes in his glory, and all the angels with him, then he will sit on his glorious throne. Before him will be gathered all the nations, and he will separate them one from another as a shepherd separates the sheep from the goats, and he will place the sheep at his right hand, but the goats at his left" (Matt. 25:31-33).

Jesus is saying that there will be an end of history, when all the world ("the nations") will be called to account for what men have done in the course of human history. Here is the end of history, when all that has happened in the centuries before will be plainly in view and understood from the point of view of God (the Son of man being Christ).

The importance of history, the life we are living from

day to day, in the eyes of God is made abundantly clear in the words of the King to the sheep on his right hand:

> "Come, O blessed of my Father, inherit the kingdom prepared for you from the foundation of the world; for I was hungry and you gave me food, I was thirsty and you gave me drink, I was a stranger and you welcomed me, I was naked and you clothed me, I was sick and you visited me, I was in prison and you came to me" (Matt. 25:34-35).

The righteous then ask the Lord when they had done all this and receive the answer: "Truly, I say to you, as you did it to one of the least of these my brethren, you did it unto me" (Matt. 25:40). The deeds of mercy and righteousness, of love and justice, which they had performed during the course of their lives were what counted in the eyes of the eternal God. The kingdom of God, which was prepared for men in the beginning ("from the foundation of the world"), will belong in the age of the ages to those who took seriously their lives between the ages. The eternal kingdom was "in the midst" of them all through their lives, even though they did not recognize it there.

It is important for us to note also that to show love and mercy, to do justly and righteously toward "the least of these my brethren," is to do it unto the Lord. All of our social action must take into account not only our own just needs and aspirations, but also the brother for whom Christ has died. This is the way in which Christ has now changed the history of the world. We can no longer do good only for the sake of the one whom we are helping; we find also that we serve Christ—consciously or unwittingly—as we do it. There is no mention here of the Church as being the exclusive heir to the kingdom of God; the test is in the lives and deeds of men performed in the middle of history. We are reminded of the words of our Lord in the Sermon on the Mount:

"Not every one who says to me, "Lord, Lord," shall enter the kingdom of heaven, but he who does the will of my Father who is in heaven" (Matt. 7:21).

THE GOOD SAMARITAN

The parable of the Good Samaritan (Luke 10:25-37) has long been a favorite proof text, both for those who believe in the Christian's responsibility for corporate social action and for those who feel this responsibility extends only to deeds of private charity. But both groups are likely to forget the fact that this parable was told by Jesus on a particular occasion to make a particular point. This point is not, as has been so often stated, that "every man is my neighbor." Neither the priest nor the Levite, although they both were offered the chance to show their bond of fellowship with a man who fell among the robbers, proved neighbor to him. It was the Samaritan, the man who took the trouble to care for him, who was his neighbor.

Here is the Bible's essential point of view clearly laid out for us to see. It cannot be stated simply as "the Fatherhood of God and the brotherhood of man," because all men do not acknowledge their relation to God and to their fellows. Yet the Bible firmly believes in the kingdom of God, the rule of God over all of life, and in the inescapable bond of society in which we all live. We all are asked to love the Lord our God with all our heart and with all our soul and with all our strength and with all our mind; and we all are asked to love our neighbor as ourself. But the choice is up to us.

Once again we see that the Bible calls for action, that it is up to us to do what God asks us to do. Jesus said to the lawyer, "Do this, and you will live" (Luke 10:28). Yet Jesus' story makes it plain that of three men who had the opportunity to show love toward the man who fell among the robbers, only one—the Samaritan whom we call "good" —acted as a neighbor toward him. Finally, when the lawyer gave the obvious answer to Jesus' question, "Which of these three, do you think, proved neighbor to the man who fell among the robbers?" Jesus said to him, "Go and do likewise" (Luke 10:36-37).

"Go and do likewise." The words speak across the centuries directly to us. Along the road of history, in this twentieth century, there are many who have fallen among robbers and been left half-dead. Poverty, hunger, and ignorance have taken their toll on some, while injustice, group superiority, and hate have stripped and beaten others. Whole nations, as well as smaller groups and individuals, have need of a neighbor who will see their need and minister to it. Will we pass by on the other side? Or will we *prove* neighbor? It is what we do, not what we believe, that will show this, for we are the ones to whom Jesus is saying, "Go and do likewise."

BUT THE GREATEST OF THESE IS LOVE

The Bible's call for action, however, is not a demand that we screw up our wills to perform heroic deeds of justice and mercy, for that is not the way that mercy is shown or justice gets done. Jesus Christ has not only taught men to prove themselves neighbor to their fellows; he has shown us how by his own life and death, and he has given us the power to do likewise through the power of his resurrection.

> "While we were yet helpless, at the right time Christ died for the ungodly. Why, one will hardly die for a righteous man—though perhaps for a good man one will dare even to die. But God shows his love for us in that while we were yet sinners Christ died for us. . . . For if while we were enemies we were reconciled to God by the death of his Son, much more, now that we are reconciled, shall we be saved by his life. Not only so, but we also rejoice in God through

our Lord Jesus Christ, through whom we have now received our reconciliation" (Rom. 5:6-8, 10-11).

We can reconcile, because we have been reconciled to God; we can share in the work of redemption, because we are redeemed; we can love, because he first loved us.

Our action is never so simple as it seems. We prefer to see it from the outside, to describe its techniques and effects. But the Bible reads us from the inside; the Bible searches the heart and speaks the word of God to us. Now that God has revealed himself to us in Jesus Christ, we know how basic love is in his nature and how central reconciliation is in his dealings with men. Knowing this, the apostle Paul could speak boldly and scathingly:

> "If I speak in the tongues of men and of angels, but have not love, I am a noisy gong or a clanging cymbal. And if I have prophetic powers, and understand all mysteries and all knowledge, and if I have all faith, so as to remove mountains, but have not love, I am nothing. If I give away all I have, and if I deliver my body to be burned, but have not love, I gain nothing" (1 Cor. 13:1-3).

Our noblest deeds of mercy and justice are as naught, if they do not have a part with the reconciling love of God.

Paul concludes his discourse on love in this way:

> "So faith, hope, love abide, these three; but the greatest of these is love" (1 Cor. 13:13).

Our faith in Jesus Christ can help us to respond to God, whose kingdom is in our very midst. Our hope that this age and all the ages to come belong to God and to his Son can give us confidence to act boldly. But it is love—divine love shown to us and all men in the offering up of our Lord Jesus Christ, and our own dim mirroring of that love in the action we take from day to day—that truly abides. This love is God's final word to us and to all men. "The greatest of these is love."

A Prayer

For a Share in the Work of Redemption

"O God, thou great Redeemer of mankind, our hearts are tender in the thought of thee, for in all the afflictions of our race thou hast been afflicted, and in the sufferings of thy people it was thy body that was crucified. Thou hast been wounded by our transgressions and bruised by our iniquities, and all our sins are laid at last on thee. Amid the groaning of creation we behold thy spirit in travail till the sons of God shall be born in freedom and holiness.

"We pray thee, O Lord, for the graces of a pure and holy life that we may no longer add to the dark weight of the world's sin that is laid upon thee, but may share with thee in thy redemptive work. As we have thirsted with evil passions to the destruction of men, do thou fill us now with hunger and thirst for justice that we may bear glad tidings to the poor and set at liberty all who are in the prison-house of want and sin. Lay thy spirit upon us and inspire us with a passion of Christ-like love that we may join our lives to the weak and oppressed and may strengthen their cause by bearing their sorrows. And if the evil that is threatened turns to smite us and if we must learn the dark malignity of sinful power, comfort us by the thought that thus we are bearing in our body the marks of Jesus, and that only those who share in his free sacrifice shall feel the plenitude of thy life.

"Help us in patience to carry forward the eternal cross of thy Christ, counting it joy if we, too, are sown as grains of wheat in the furrows of the world, for only by the agony of the righteous comes redemption. Amen."

—Walter Rauschenbusch.[1]

[1] From *Prayers of the Social Awakening* by Walter Rauschenbusch, pp. 117-118. Published by The Pilgrim Press. Used by permission.

For Your Personal Meditation and Study

Galatians 3:23—4:7. What do you think Paul means when he says that God sent his Son "when the time had fully come"? Does this have any connection with Jesus' insistence that he came to "fulfill" the law and the prophets? (See Chap. 3.)

Romans 8:18-25. What is "the hope" in which Paul says we were saved? Why is he so certain that "hope that is seen is not hope"?

Revelation 21:1-8 (cf. Isa. 65:17-25). Why do these passages in speaking about the future mention "a new heaven *and* a new earth" rather than heaven only? What is the significance of the future being presented as like a city? In what ways is the life described like the life we know? In what ways is it different?

Matthew 25:31-46. What has this passage meant to you in the past? Is there anything you see in it now that you had not noticed before?

Luke 10:29-37. In what way does Jesus' parable answer the lawyer's question? Did the Samaritan perform his kindness as an act of personal charity? Can social action be considered a form of "proving neighbor"?

1 Corinthians 13:1-13. Why does Paul consider love greater than faith or hope? Does he mean that we should not work for others, when he says that giving away all we have or delivering our body to be burned—without love—is nothing?

For Thought and Discussion

1. What facts do you and your friends take for granted about time?

2. What is the difference between a future eternity that is timeless and one that extends "to the age of the ages"?

3. History is of importance to God. Are there any particular ages of history that are of greater importance than others in the sight of God? Is there any particular period in the life of our own time that has special significance to God?

4. Give examples of the Greek view of history as an endless succession of cycles; of the progress theory; and of the golden age theory. In what ways is the Christian view of time different?

5. How is it possible for us as Christians to work together with people who do not see time in the same way that we do?

6. What can we reasonably hope for when we undertake to improve society through social action? What can we not hope for? Is our work meaningless because we must work in hope?

7. Give examples of individualistic views of the future life. Do you agree that this future life is the life of a community and not merely immortality for the individual?

8. Can the Christian know as he works that God will approve what he is doing and will cause his work to endure?

9. Can all of the ills of the world be cured by personal charity, as in Jesus' story of the Samaritan's gracious deed? If other means are needed, what are they?

10. Is the Christian the only one who can know and show the kind of love Paul writes about in 1 Corinthians 13? Do all Christians manifest this kind of love in their lives?